The Delicious

A Companion to
New Food Culture

gestalten

BORRELBITES
TASTING PLATTERS

Taking a Bite Out of Preface a Tastier World

BY GIULIA PINES

When we look back on the most important moments of our lives, all have certain features that make them hard to forget: The childhood birthday party when all our school friends were invited, the graduation that marked our first step into adulthood; our weddings, anniversaries, holidays, and New Year's Eve celebrations. The birthday parties of our own children, with all their school friends invited. When we look back on these occasions, recount them to friends, and recreate them in our minds, too often it is not the décor we remember. It is not what we wore. It is not even which of our loved ones were there; although we can recall a feeling of comfort and happiness, try as we might, perhaps we will not remember which aunt, uncle, or grandparent was present. When we conjure up the most beautiful details that make up our most fondly remembered events, we very often think of the food. Who hasn't caught himself regaling friends with tales of an elaborate wedding he just attended, only to realize he is mostly thinking about the cake? Who doesn't remember the trays of cookies baked at Christmas, the crunchy, salty snacks and refreshing drinks brought to a picnic, or the unforgettable meal that was the highlight of a once-in-a-lifetime trip? Science tells us that our sense of smell is inextricably linked with memory, but what if our sense of taste is too? We hardly let an important milestone in our lives go by without eating something delicious.

Beyond this seemingly primordial desire to commemorate with food is an even more startling revelation: over the last decade or so, food has become not just a means of nourishing ourselves or throwing a good party; it has become pastime, passion, and politics. Scratch the surface of any major issue—be it world poverty, cultural assimilation versus preservation, immigration, climate change and sustainability, or economics—and you'll find that food plays a role. A growing number of companies large and small have emerged to champion environmental issues through their approaches to food: if the problem is global warming, the solution is organic farming on a small-scale, foodsharing projects that do double duty in eliminating excess waste by giving leftovers to the hungry, restaurants that champion vegetarianism not just as a means of ending animal cruelty, but as a way of curbing excess CO2 produced by factory farming, and community initiatives that educate the public on healthy and sustainable eating practices. Although we are often quick to single out technology as the enemy here, high-tech solutions—zero-energy agriculture, lab-grown meat, machines that can cook,

or even 3D-printed food — may be the answer to feeding an exploding world population.

Perhaps in response to increasing globalization and our dependence on ever more powerful forms of technology, however, a growing number of people are eschewing technology and anonymous sources of overly processed foods by finding themselves again — in the kitchen. Old recipes are being reinvented with fervor as a great many passionate food lovers become home picklers, brewers, bakers, and chefs. Cooking a meal at home for friends has become the height of refinement — a way to show that you have the skills, the know-how, and the appreciation to make a meal that is far more personal, and perhaps far more delicious, than anything a restaurant might serve. These days, you are just as likely to keep up with cooking and dining trends as you are to stay up-to-date with global current events. Today, everyone is a bon vivant, to be in-the-know is to be a foodie, and eating has become the way we broadcast our knowledge of culture, our respect for tradition, and our lust for the good life.

Food has always been a means of crossing boundaries and creating understanding on a deeply local level.

In the past few years, food has become inextricably linked with travel as well. No sooner do you announce your upcoming vacation destination than a barrage of restaurant recommendations follow. Questions of where and what you ate linger long after your return. Eating well on a trip used to be associated with the predictable destinations — France, Italy, and Spain, for instance — now it can just as easily be a reason for planning a trip in the first place.

But why is it so important that we eat well when we are away from home? After all, we cannot bring back what we've eaten, and there are arguably better ways to spend time and money when abroad. Perhaps it is part of the swelling

backlash against materialistic culture we are seeing worldwide. Although a large part of our travels — and our meals while traveling — are documented using up-to-date technology with increasing frequency (we find a restaurant with the Yelp app, make a reservation via Foursquare, take pictures of our meal and post them on Instagram), enjoying food is a way of recapturing time for ourselves, grounding ourselves in the here and now and showing others that we can appreciate the genuine moments in life. What is more, using our travel time to go on the hunt for a meal is somehow both hedonistic and nihilistic — we are not having the travel experiences our parents and grandparents might have had — full of museums, shopping, and planned activities — we are making our own way. At its heart, it is an excuse to set ourselves apart from the pack when we travel, to chase down the ever-coveted sense of authenticity and belonging so much of travel is about anyway.

And sometimes, we do bring some of it back with us, enlightening friends about delicious new places we have visited, and changing opinions as we go. It is perhaps no surprise that a few of the regions earning the most attention right now are somewhat politically controversial: food has always been a means of crossing boundaries and creating understanding on a deeply local level, and as most foodies' tastes, interests, and obsessions are already distinctly international, it makes sense

that they would look beyond politics to get to the true heart of a place, which very often beats in its kitchens.

In turn, when travelers come home with a newfound interest in cuisines they may have known nothing about, they start combing the streets in their own cities and neighborhoods, looking for what they so dearly miss. How many visitors to China, for example, have ended up in the Chinatowns of New York, San Francisco, or London, trying to suss out the savory treats that bring back memories of their trip? How many visitors to Peru return home wanting to replicate the amazing ceviche and Pisco cocktails they had there?

For that matter, how much of Peruvian cuisine was influenced by a late nineteenth century wave of Japanese immigrants trying to recreate the feeling of home through food? Some are content to search until they find what they are looking for; others do it themselves, opening restaurants, starting supper-clubs, or powering up food trucks to peddle delicacies that lovingly replicate their food travels. Cross-border cultural outreach is no small feat, and if it can be accomplished with something baked, grilled or fried, then why not?

This cultural obsession with food has also found expression in a new approach to products. What may have been a simple trip to the supermarket in the past has now become a distinct expression of self; dietary preferences, political leanings, cultural background, fitness and health levels, all of it can now be reflected in the simple act of reaching for one product over another at the grocery store. We want to know our products have been made the right way — by people, not machines — and more than that, we want to know they have a story, a background, a creation myth. Simply put, we want

our food products to be more like us — nuanced, complicat-ed, and full of character; connected to an entire network of humans who have helped raise and nurture them. All due respect to Willy Wonka, but his chocolate factory wouldn't stand a chance in the twenty-first century; he'd have to open an artisanal, small-batch chocolate shop instead.

Most of these products place a high emphasis on unadul-terated nutrition; organic, raw, vegan, and paleo are all catch-phrases that tell us what we are buying and eating has some-how passed muster — whether by us or by society at a large. That's why the juices we buy so often come labeled as cold pressed, the coffee we look for is fair trade, and the eggs we want most for our morning omelets are cage-free. Packaging has also risen to the challenge, reflecting a cleverness and a conscientious melding of design and function like never before; nowadays, a food company is just as likely to work with a local artist to design its packaging as it is to consult a branding expert. Products are no longer simple items to be thrown in a shopping cart, but rather important, tangible forms of consumer outreach. Aided by visual art and story-telling, companies are building relationships with customers in entirely new ways.

And if chefs are the new rockstars, then it would make sense that adoring fans would follow their every move. Today, we have seen an explosion in cookbook publishing like never before; while print media stagnates, the cookbook table at your local bookstore is beginning to groan under the weight of the many tomes written by and about chefs. As the econ-omy continues to recover from an economic crisis, the num-bers of people willing to spend good money on a good meal continues to increase. Food festivals have a higher attendance than music festivals, and even the art and fashion worlds are trying to get in on the action. Edible installations dig deep into the meaning of food in society, edible creations show-case an unbelievable amount of skill, precision, and collective

work hours; both are now a specialty of many top artists and designers. Fashion models post their home-cooked meals on social media, and healthy food and lifestyle bloggers are revered as much as fashion models.

Where can all of this lead? It would be easy to dismiss the new obsession with food as a trend like any other—something that will come and go without a trace, as we return to our microwave dinners, processed breakfast cereals, and fast food meals. But cultivating an interest in food is not like buying a new pair of jeans or even curating an expert record collection. It is a consumer activity that nonetheless results in nothing left to consume, its trappings purely materialistic but ultimately perishable. Food is something we take an interest in not just because we can, but because we absolutely must. It is a hobby, a passion, and one of the purest building blocks of life. Good thing it's also delicious.

Playing with Your Food

Innovative and Playful Concepts for Fun and Tasty Eating

Ever since the over-the-top, decadent banquets that eventually brought Louis XVI and Marie Antoinette to the guillotine during the French Revolution, presentation has played a significant part in what we eat, how we see what we eat, and how the chefs who prepare what we eat show off their consummate skills. Nowadays, however, the realm of high-end food presentation is no longer left to the dining halls of monarchs and millionaires; food designers of all stripes are capturing the imagination by approaching food not just as something to eat, but as an art form in and of itself—a powerful evocation of nostalgia, excitement, and curiosity.

Many of these designers manage to be playful and thought provoking at the same time, serving edible creations that are nice to look at and no doubt delicious, but also connect to a theme or reference an idea. Tour de Fork, a self-proclaimed Culinary Creative Consultancy, sticks to the fanciful side of things with their project "Finger Food," commissioned by Italian magazine *CASAfacile*. Laser-cut rings

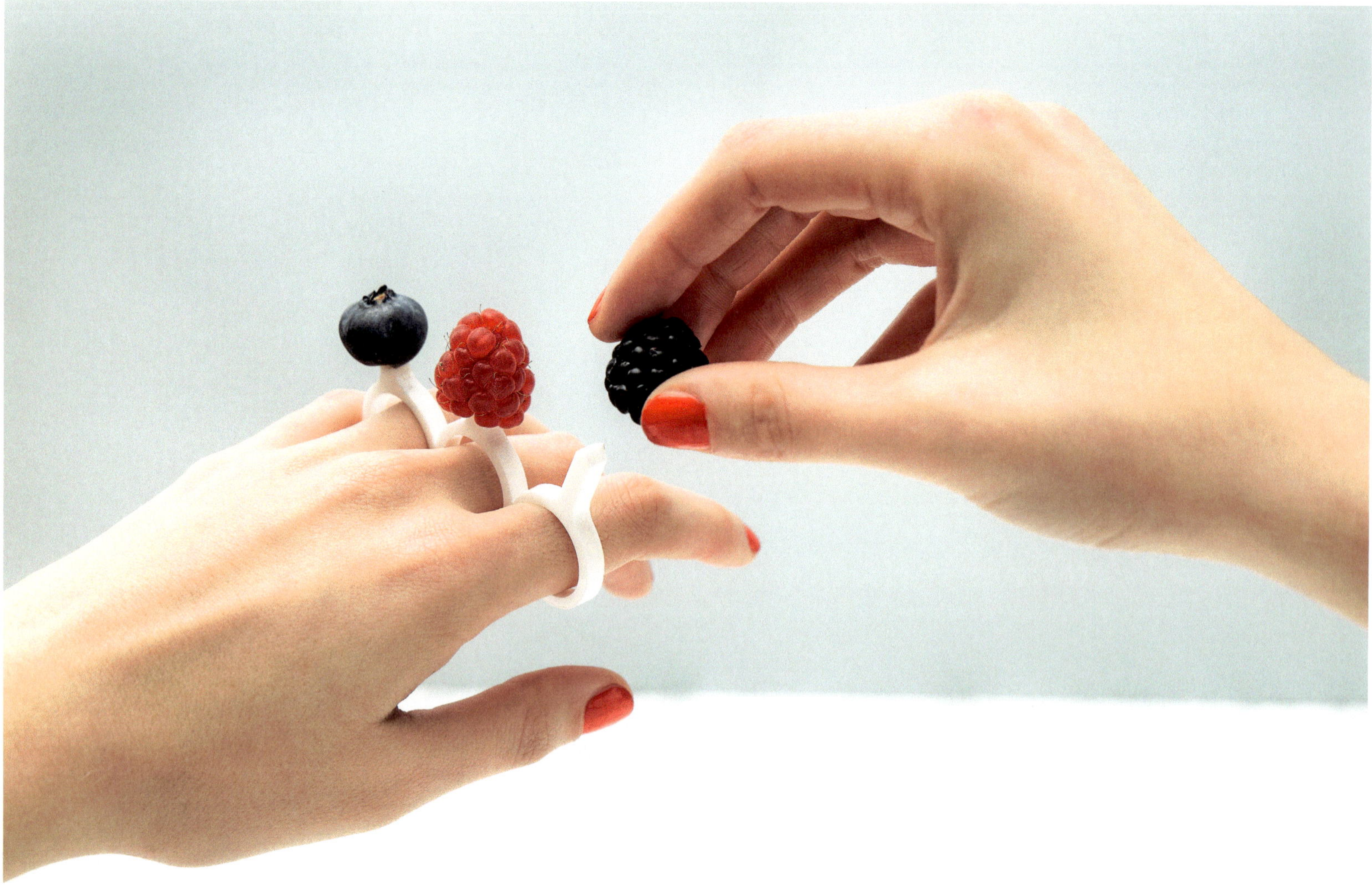

Tour de Fork's 3D-printed rings can be decorated with jewel-like berries.

of various design are made for specific use with food: they can be adorned with pieces of fruit, petit fours, chocolates, or even, if you want to get cheeky, cheese and crackers and other savory delights. Reclaiming the idea of finger food in the most literal way possible, Tour de Fork makes laser cutting accessible and fun to the average consumer, while also capturing the excitement of a children's tea party and updating it for adults.

Meanwhile, Jinhyun Jeon, a South Korean-born, Netherlands-based designer, is adding a spark of playfulness and an element of surprise to what has long been seen as a staid, serious, and fairly predictable art: cutlery. For centuries, the design of fine dishware and expert cutlery has perhaps been considered just as important as cooking, food preparation, and presentation. Now, by taking an object as simple as the spoon and elongating it, painting it, ribbing it with nubs and spokes, giving it a rougher, grainer texture, or deepening its bowl, Jeon has added new layers of perception to a ritual we all take part in, regardless of age, nationality, or social status: eating a meal.

With synesthesia in mind – the condition in which the human senses mix and match to create new perceptions, tasting music,

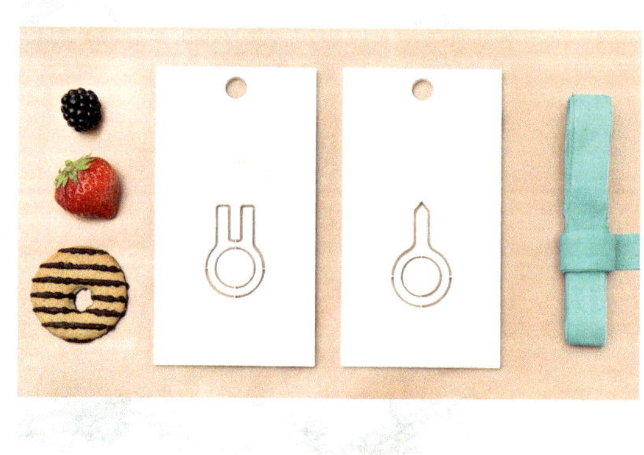

Finger Food

*

ABOUT: *"A collection of laser cut rings that can be decorated with small cakes, fruit, or candy. Once you have finished playing with your food, it's ready to be eaten and enjoyed, without waste."*

for example, or hearing color—Jeon pushes the boundaries of tableware, questioning what it can add to the experience of eating. As the artist herself says, "The tableware we use for eating should not just be a tool for placing food in our mouths; it should become an extension of our body, challenging our senses even in the moment when the food is still on its way to be-ing consumed."

By concentrating on the tools we use to bring food to our mouths—an oft-overlooked compo-nent of the eating experience—Jeon directs our attention to the sensory stimuli that make up this experience, which she says can include not only taste as it is understood in the convention-al way, but also elements of temperature, color, texture, volume or weight, and form. How hot or cold an edible item is can have a ⟫

Jinhyun Jeon's surreal cutlery alters the eating experience.

Eindhoven, Netherlands
Jinhyun Jeon

*

ABOUT: *Cutlery design focuses on getting food from plate to mouth, but it could do so much more. Inspired by synesthesia, this project aims to push the limits of what tableware can do.*

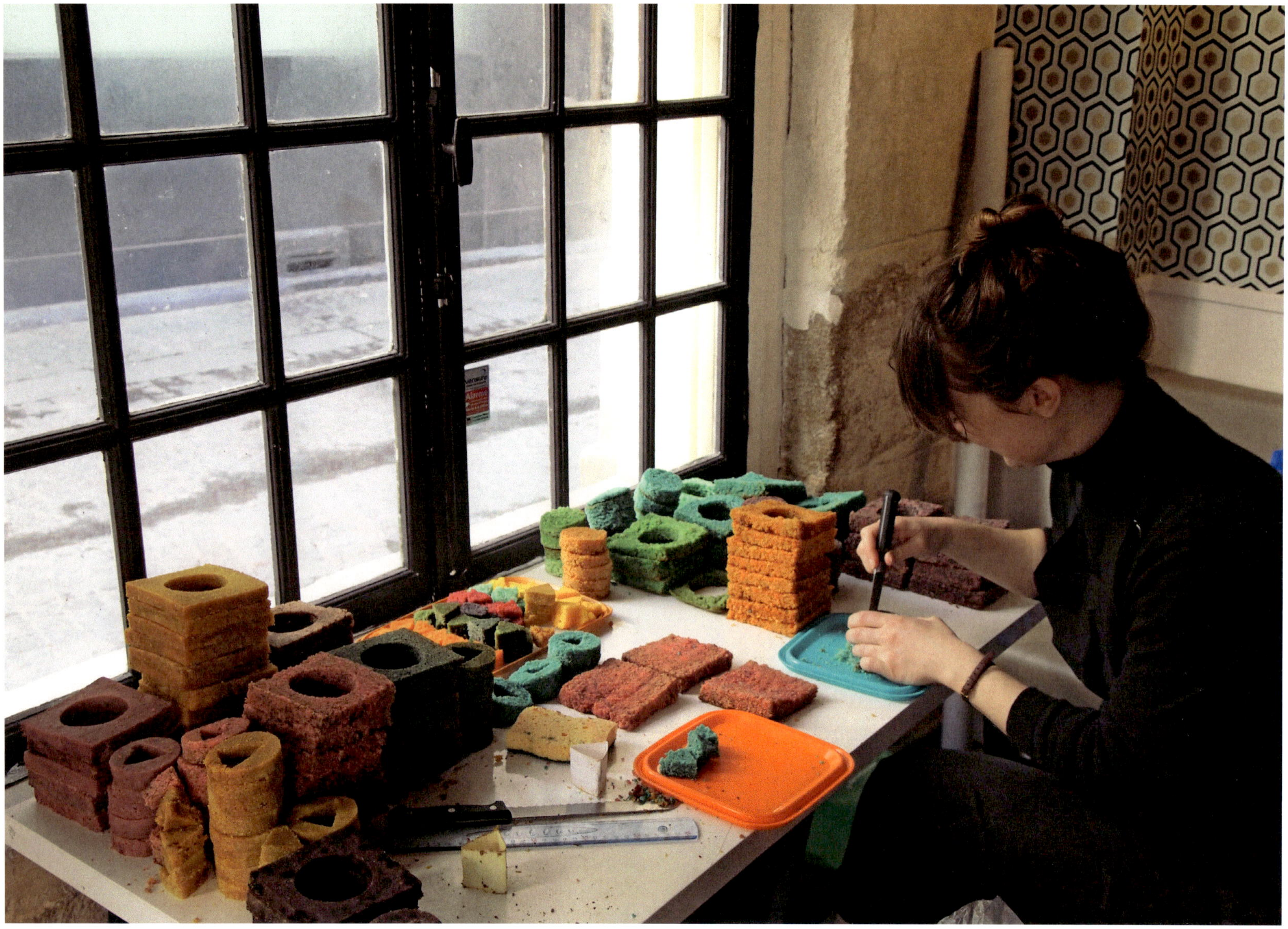

profound effect on how we experience it, and as a utensil becomes lighter, we disconcertingly begin to perceive the true weight of the food we consume, instead of the fork or spoon that holds it. What is more, since each person's "tongue map" is unique, with different areas corresponding to different tastes and sensations, each person's interaction with Jeon's cutlery will be unique and irreproducible.

Sonia Verguet, projects whimsy and childlike wonder as she makes connections between food and other walks of life.

Strasbourg-based food designer Sonia Verguet, projects whimsy and childlike wonder as she makes connections between food and other walks of life. A delicate dusting of powdered sugar atop a Christmas cake is interrupted by the soft imprint of tiny birds' feet. Lines of musical notes reveal themselves to be edible cookies, each a different flavor to represent jazz, pop, rock, and electro. Edible floor tiles and herringbone parquet are a playful, adult homage to "Hansel and Gretel." Children at a science museum are encouraged to become archeologists, searching through a mound of shortbread earth to find dinosaur bone cookies and connect them to form skeletons. Everything is edible, everything is playful and interactive, and by inviting participation from those who engage with her creations, she encourages her audience to think differently about the role food plays in our culture — how it is used to celebrate or commemorate, to mark important life events or simply the changing of the seasons.

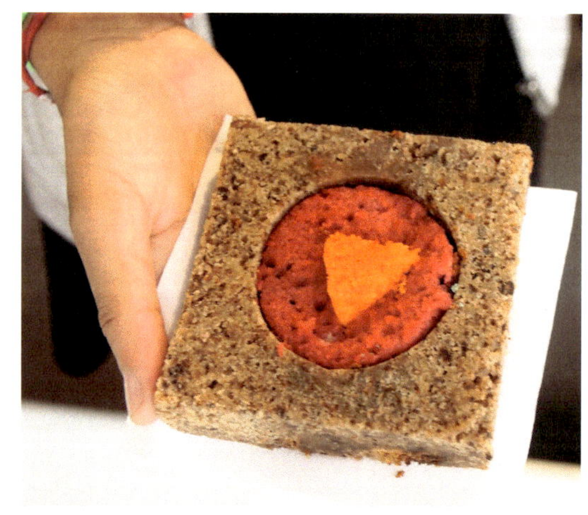

Many of Sonia Verguet's playful designs are meant to evoke the wonders of childhood.

Strasbourg, France.

Sonia Verguet

*

ABOUT: _Playful, interactive food exhibitions and installations that serve to teach us about our relationship with what we eat while invoking a playful, childlike wonder at all things edible._

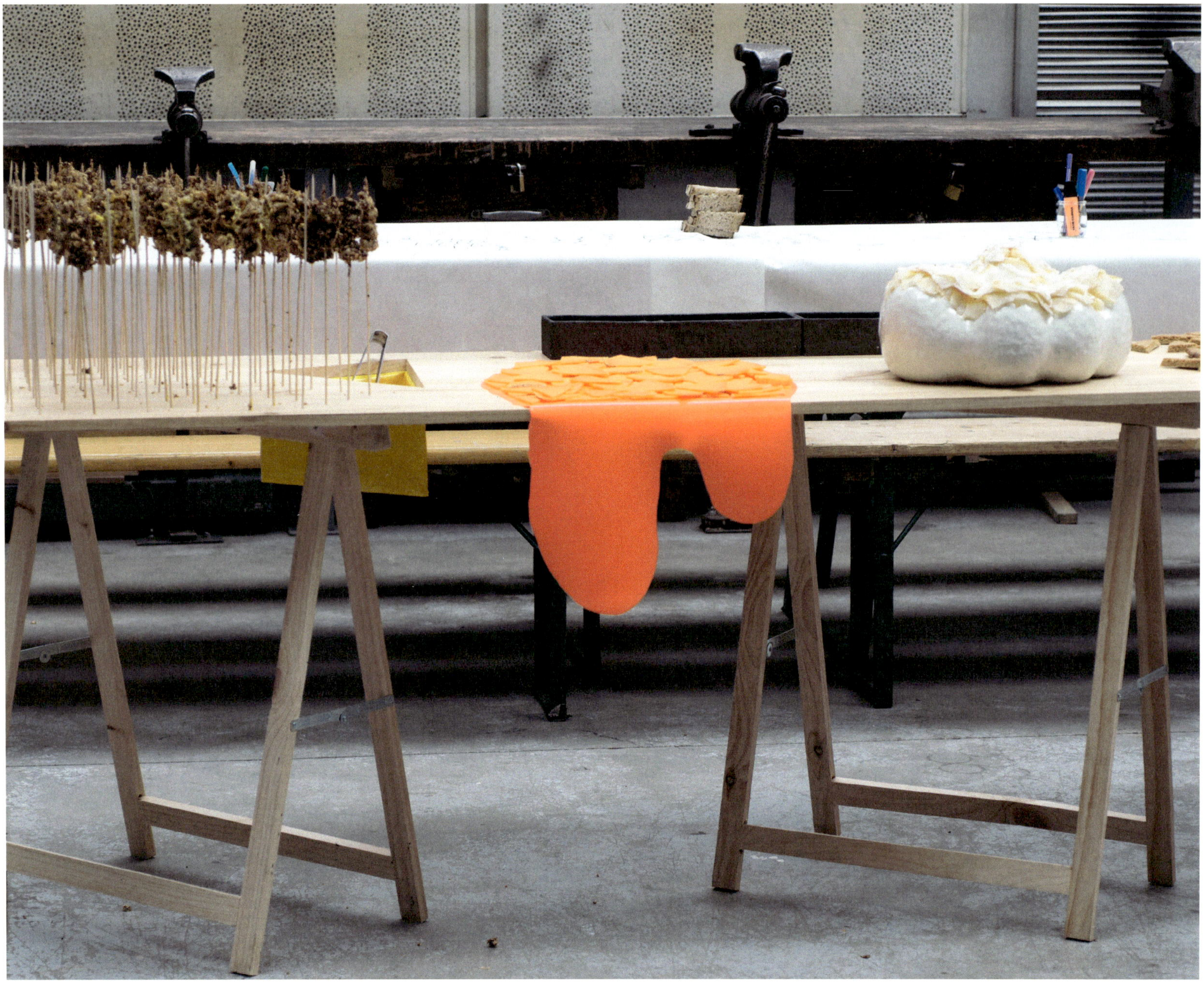

Encouraging us to think differently about the role food plays in our culture.

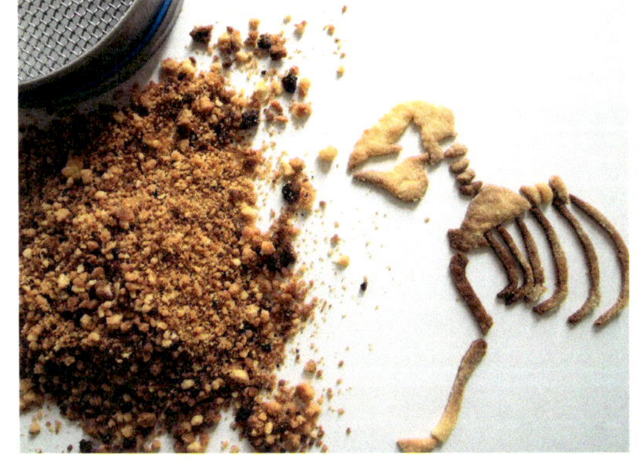

Verguet's work provides the most striking and memorable component to gallery openings or magazine launches, sparks children's interest in museums by creating delicious, hands-on exhibition components, and prompts a reevaluation of everyday objects. That Christmas cake, for example, is meant to evoke the wonder of an unexpected but long-awaited snowfall on Christmas day – a quiet moment of joy to cut through the stress of holiday preparations. The edible notes are an attempt to talk about music – a subject that has exhausted the limits of language by now – in a new way for the 25th anniversary of the music festival Les Eurockéennes.

Approaching food in a different but nonetheless playfully intellectual way is Studio Appétit, helmed by designer and chef Ido Garini. Using food, dishware, and the act of cooking to create

Sonia Verguet's edible houses are a play on the term homemade.

multisensory experiences, Garini and his team aim to elevate food design to a level that has since been reserved for the worlds of fashion and art. The whimsical work, "Luscious Food Cravings," for example, uses a series of porcelain cones to present edible items as if they were high-end pieces in a jewelry shop; much like Tour de Fork's Finger Food rings, this conceptual installation presents things to eat as if they were objets d'art, at the same time asking why they have not earned the same level of reverence as a diamond bauble. The "Bellboy Dining Concept" turns the act of dining into an eclectic cabinet of curiosities, with some edible objects that make sense, and some, like a cuckoo clock or a miniature bathtub with accompanying rubber ducky, that do not fit at all, evoking a Dada-esqe brush with absurdist fantasy. Studio Appétit's goal is clear: to make you question the norm when it comes to food while giving you an appetite for the extraordinary.

Chocolataria Equador, which despite its name is based in Porto, Portugal, takes food design in a more traditional direction,

crafting intricate and impressive chocolate creations fit for a royal table—some of them extravagant enough that they could indeed have shown up at the banquet of Madamoiselle Antoinette herself. "Each product is the result of a small story that happens in the Vila do Lago, a small village inspired by the Douro Valley in Portugal, where the days run slowly, and where our dreams and flavours find the right place," explain founders Celestino Fonseca and Teresa Almeida of one of their whimsical projects. "We value an historic legacy expressed in not only the shapes and colors but also the dreamed up flavors of a Portuguese world, in which cacao assumes a privileged place."

To that end, customers encounter tiny chocolate praline squares engraved with stripes, flowers, and intricate leaf designs, chocolate eggs filled with nuts and dried fruits that might rival the wildest creations of Fabergé, chocolate Christmas trees and wintry villages touched with a snowy dusting of powdered sugar, and tableaux overflowing with white

Porto, Portugal
Chocolataria Equador

*

ABOUT: *"We value an historic legacy expressed not only in shapes and colours, but also in the dreamed of flavours of a Portuguese world in which cacao assumes a privileged place."*

Chocolataria Equador's creations are meant to evoke nostalgia, playfulness, and the art of classic chocolate-making.

Master Chocolatier Miguel Tedim

Studio Appétit

*

ABOUT: *A multidisciplinary experience design studio specializing in food design and culinary projects, utilizing uncharted territories to create and enhance multisensory experiences.*

Studio Appétit

*

Studio Appétit's creations make you question the norm while giving you an appetite for the extraordinary.

dark chocolate "walnuts," "cones," and "shells." A white chocolate disc on a stick becomes nearly too beautiful to eat with the addition of an exquisite bird-and-flower miniature that appears almost Persian-inspired. Meanwhile, the shop is like a vision of days gone by, its brick and wood interior with arched, cave-like ceilings and tiled floors evocative of old Europe—where your grandparents' grandparents might have gone to buy gifts for the whole family before returning home from an extravagant Grand Tour.

These designers and producers realize the value in elevating food from something to be merely physically consumed to a delicacy. Something consumed with all the senses and, above all,

DO NOT FEED
THE HIPPOS!

BELLBOY
BAR

Elevating food to a delicacy: something consumed with all the senses—and, above all, with the intellect.

with the intellect. Cooking, baking, and food preparation of all sorts have long been referred to as the culinary arts. With their creative, whimsical, and somewhat brilliant offerings, these culinary innovators seem to be saying, "Let's abandon the pretense and actually make it so: food is art, and that is how it should be."

London, England
Catherine Losing

*

ABOUT: *Taking your mom's favourite*
expression "The dinner is not going to cook itself!"
into a whole new realm of possibility.

Cathering Losing's wacky installations ask: can these food items cook themselves?

Playing with your food. It's something we are told time and time again as children not to do. Yet photographer Catherine Losing has come up with a playful way of experimenting with food that may make parents think twice about letting kids get their hands on their dinners. Collaborating with Iain Graham for the U.K. food and culture journal *The Gourmand,* the two set up a series of absurdist tableaux that turn the idea of the still life on its head, all based on the concept that food is capable of conducting electricity, and therefore, preposterously, perhaps of even cooking itself.

Inspired by the idea of the potato clock—an experiment many kids may have conducted either in a school science lab or at home to show that chemical reactions within something as mundane as the potato create enough electricity to power a clock—Losing and Graham hooked up raw fish and fowl with a variety of clips, wires, tubes, and chains, creating something that is part mad scientist run amok, part torture chamber.

And who are the protagonists of these macabre images, not yet gory, but with the express implication of carnage? A dead

Lumps of chicken parts, coxcombed head and feet recognizable but not much else in between.

octopus hung from a hook, one skinny, slimy leg wrapped around an electric saw no doubt seconds away from cleanly dismembering itself. Lumps of chicken parts, coxcombed head, and feet recognizable but not much else in between, sitting next to a fryer as if awaiting their fate, while presided over by raw, red, indignant pigs' eyeballs. Plates of gloppy berries and cream, perched precariously on white chocolate plates melting in front of a space heater they themselves are ostensibly powering. An electric eel with cables clipped at either end, ready to show off just how much electricity it can really generate.

Beyond creating a collection of unsettling images, the two are perhaps unwittingly making a statement about our culture's obsession with those perfectly styled, mouthwatering pictures of food too flawless for you ever to make at home, now showing up everywhere from amateur cooking blogs to the pages of prestigious food magazines (and even the pages of this book).

Short Stack Editions

*

ABOUT: *A series of small-format cookbooks authored by America's top culinary talents. Each edition is a collectible, single-subject booklet offering ingenious new ways to cook our favorite ingredients.*

S hort Stack Editions are small-format cookbook periodicals funded by a Kickstarter campaign—a perfect melding of pre-Internet DIY creativity and twenty-first century social media. Each of Short Stack's small, hand-bound volumes celebrates one ingredient: a playful or elegant print of it adorns the cover, while its pages are filled with meticulously tested recipes and personal tips. Of course, the books are also written by exactly the types of people you would want writing about food: cookbook authors, food magazine editors, and other food industry professionals who balance diligence, passion, and a bit of obsession in both life and work.

The cover of *Eggs*, for example, written by long-time *Gourmet* editor Ian Knauer, is polka-dotted by white eggs and yoke-colored shadows; a simple but appealing retro design evocative of childhood breakfasts. For *Strawberries*, graphic, symmetrical cross-sections of the fruits line up like arrowheads, while the wheel-like citrus slices adorning *Lemons* have an almost Art Deco sensibility. *Brown Sugar* features futuristic crystals floating in space, and the red-and-white marbling on *Prosciutto di Parma*, overlaid with a grid of grey triangles, manages to be both elegant and meaty.

These are no magazines, but rather snippets of an author's brain as he or she riffs on a particular food. So there are no advertisers taking up pages with glossy images of how life should be but rarely is, no stylized spreads with recipes

Short Stack's handmade recipe books each glorify a single product.

you could never possibly achieve at home, no pictures of celebrity kitchens to compare, unfavorably, to your own — just one food lover's passion for a product, communicated to another food lover in a series of lovingly illustrated pages. The designs spark a strong feeling of nostalgia mixed with curiosity to catch the attention of average bookstore browsers. Perhaps after taking a look, they'll realize their knowledge of everyday ingredients like apples, honey, corn, or tomatoes is coming up a bit, well, short. Luckily, Short Stack is here to help with that.

Just one food lover's passion for a product, communicated to another.

MATH. ADING. SUCCESS.
KUMON

New York City, NY, USA

Table for Two

*

ABOUT: *Shani Ha plays with the context and vocabulary of the restaurant by twisting an archetypal bistro table into an interactive installation.*

Two strangers communicating through a screen in Shani Ha's New York City installation: a symbol of our times?

The Paris-born, New York-based artist Shani Ha says it all when she states, "New York is a very crowded city, yet so many people are alone." Her interactive installation *Table for Two* is an effort to highlight this gap while also bridging it. In fact, the entire world is very crowded these days, but so many people are alone. That's because the twenty-first century has seen the proliferation of computers, tablets, and smartphones—daily companions that have superseded all need for human contact and become the only friends we feel we need.

Table for Two, which was installed at the West Village intersection of 7th Avenue and Carmine Street in downtown Manhattan, offers passers-by, onlookers, and participants a chance at a moment outside of time; an encounter with a stranger over a cup of tea. The table, positioned half inside and half outside a glass-walled establishment (actually a real restaurant: AYZA Wine & Chocolate Bar) is both inviting and off-putting; at night it recalls nothing less than the iconic Edward Hopper work *Nighthawks*, which also invoked a certain loneliness and world-weariness that can only be attributed to modern urban life. In this particular tableau, however, the characters have a choice: They can sit at the table alone, watching their own reflection in the glass much as they might see an image of themselves reflected back at them through their use of social media or the glow of a reflective computer screen. If they sit with a companion, or accept the tacit invitation of a person on the other side of the glass, they may have a spontaneous and enjoyable experience based on wholly unplanned interaction—less

and less frequent these days, what with the virtual worlds we increasingly inhabit.

The message of isolation versus interaction is clear, but there is a certain poetry to the delivery. Since Shani Ha comes from Paris, New York's lightning quick, coffee-to-go, career-oriented, time-is-money culture must have been startling, even alienating to her. This project is no doubt an attempt to get back to her roots in France—a country that still somewhat appreciates a calm moment over a shared meal, an hour away from ambition's relentless drive. How perfect, we might think, that this encouraged authenticity takes place at a table. How fitting that we are invited to share something real over a simple cup of tea.

Edible Avant-Garde

How many scientific innovations have gone toward improving the world through food? There are obvious forerunners like Norman Borlaug, the American biologist who won the Nobel Peace Prize for engineering high-yield crops, which are estimated to have saved millions from world hunger in developing countries. There is Louis Pasteur, the French chemist and microbiologist who leant his name to a process he discovered—pasteurization—that prevents bacterial contamination in dairy products. The Glasgow-born William Cullen and the American Oliver Evans share credit for developing the first artificial refrigeration system and designing an actual refrigerator, respectively. These days, however, most of us think we have food all figured out.

But the scientific world is still hard at work behind the scenes, figuring out how to change the essential properties of what we grow, gather, prepare, and consume. In some cases, like the very public grassroots fight against the multinational agrochemical corporation Monsanto, these

Fungi Mutarium

*

scientific discoveries can backfire, making both farmers and consumers mistrust global food sources and question important innovations that have made food safe and healthy. In some cases, like the lab-grown burger that was first reported to cost 325,000 dollars, these innovations can seem downright frivolous. Still, there is a small but growing crop of innovators who are using the high-tech tools of today to create the foods of tomorrow — to surprising, thought provoking, and entertaining effect.

3D printing has been in the news lately, but it is still largely out of the reach of the average consumer. Reading about 3D printing, you might be tempted to think it belongs squarely to the realm of scientists, doctors, and techie geeks. But Los Angeles company 3D Systems Culinary is doing exactly what its name would suggest: making this technology available to culinary professionals. "These folks are already artists and innovators in their own right," says the company,

"and 3D printing will be an incredibly powerful new tool to add to their repertoires." The 3D sugar designs the company uses to promote the system, which will become commercially available in 2016, look like chemical models, children's building blocks, and works of ⟫

Utrecht, Netherlands
Fungi Mutarium

*

ABOUT: *More technologies are needed to farm under extreme environmental conditions. Fungi Mutarium cultivates edible fungal biomass on a plastic waste inside agar, seaweed based gelatin.*

<u>With their innovative project, Livin Studio cultivates edible biomass from plastic waste.</u>

St Davids, Wales

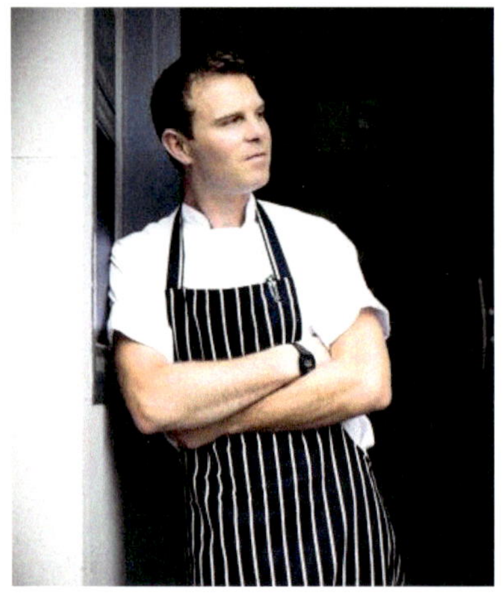

Grub Kitchen

*

ABOUT: *An innovative food business promoting and championing the practice of entomophagy (eating insects). Sustainable, seasonal and local food is paramount to Grub Kitchen's ethos.*

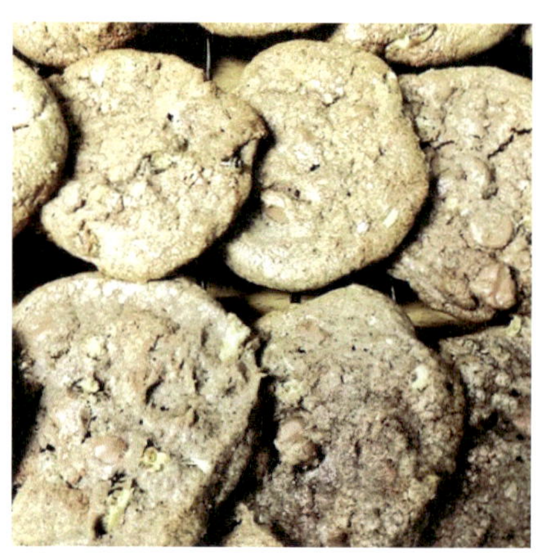

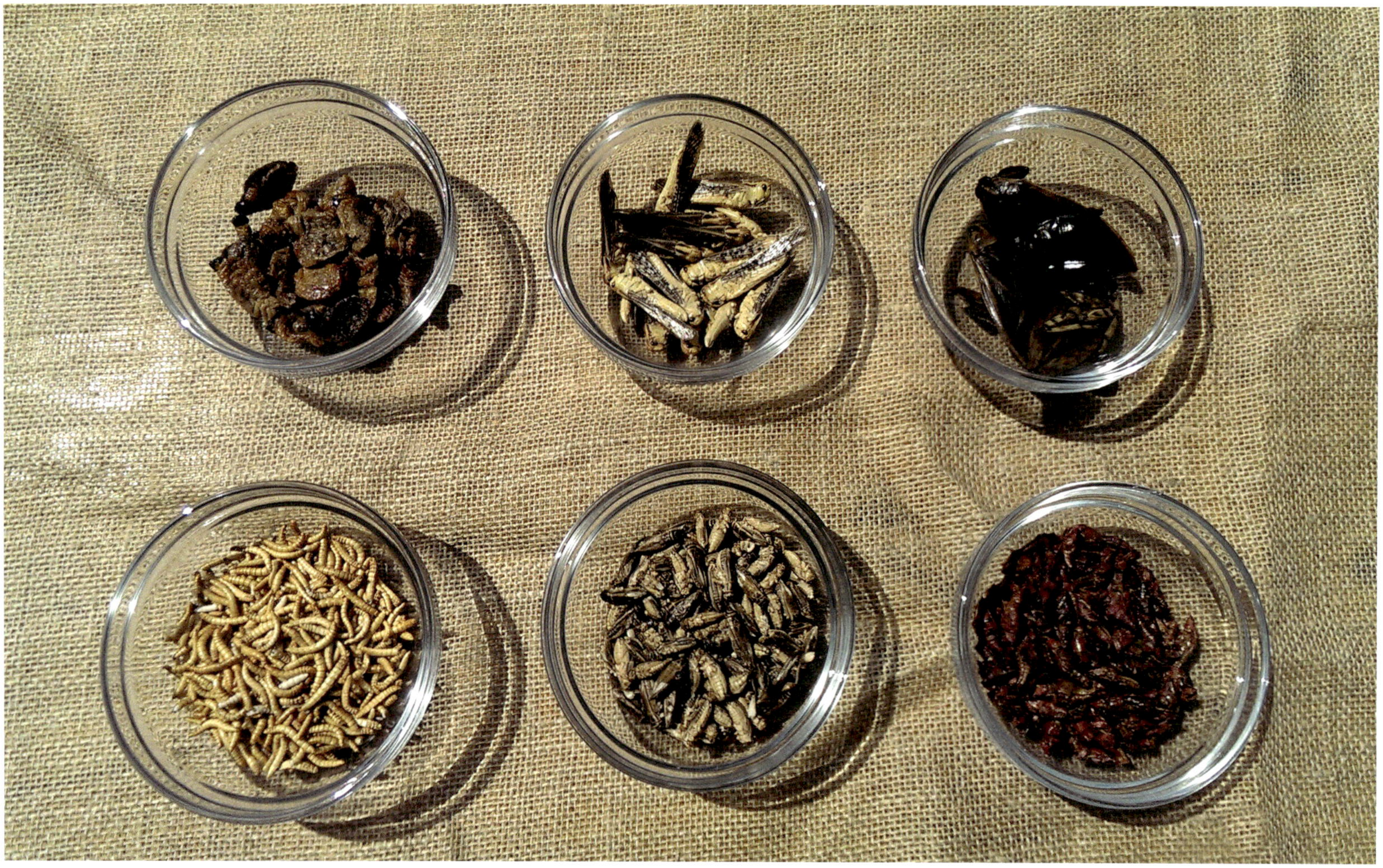

Those looking for an alternative source of protein should seriously look into things that crawl.

pop art. They can top cakes, adorn cocktails, or become the centerpiece of an elaborate party.

How does it work? "The ChefJet Pro printers use a process that's a lot like making frosting in your kitchen at home," explains the company. "It builds up a custom confection by adding the wet ingredients of the recipe to the dry ingredients, only extremely precisely, on a layer by layer basis. The ChefJet Pro also has the ability to incorporate food coloring into each layer of the sweet during the printing process, so that the printed confection emerges in full, photographic quality color."

Dutch designer Chloé Rutzerveld uses 3D printing in another way, envisioning it as the start of an innovative process she calls "Edible Growth," rather than the main act. "Edible growth is an example of a future food product that forms a bridge between new technologies and authentic practices of growing and breeding food," she explains. "Multiple layers containing an edible breeding ground, seeds, spores, and yeast are printed according to a personalized 3D file, after which natural processes like photosynthesis and fermentation will start. Within five days the plants and fungi mature." The result is a strange but somehow quaint

Farm 432

*

ABOUT: *Freedom from the current meat production system by growing our own protein source. After 432 hours, one gram of black soldier fly eggs turn into 2.4 kilos of larvae protein.*

ChefJet Pro

*

ABOUT: *The first professional-grade culinary 3D printer, appropriate for bakers, pastry chefs, molecular gastronomists, and mixologists.*

little biosphere consisting of an edible base, a soil, and plant and fungi matter that looks like something space explorers might have eaten on another planet in a sci-fi film from the 1960s.

Oddly enough, according to Rutzerveld, the reality is much closer at hand: we may be eating these in the not-so-distant future, as scientists and food innovators continue to look for low-carbon methods of growing food in order to slow the drastic warming of the planet and feed an exploding global population. Edible Growth, says Ruzerveld, "makes smart use of natural processes like fermentation and photosynthesis and lowers the use of resources. It contributes to our and the environment's wellbeing by using this new technology in a useful way to shorten the entire food chain, with the result of a reduction in food waste, food miles, and CO2 emission."

The hope is that consumers' direct involvement in the printing and growing process will lead them to have a deeper appreciation of the food they eat, and by extension, what it takes to bring food to millions of tables worldwide.

One food that lands on many of these tables is insects. For a lot of people, entomophagy — the consumption of insects — is something they simply cannot stomach. But many cultures — notably in Mexico and parts of Southeast Asia — have been incorporating creepy-crawlies into a regular diet for years. To them, bugs are just another source of protein, but the nutritional benefits are staggering: crickets, caterpillars, and termites provide a per kilo percentage of protein on par with pigs and cows while producing far less CO2. That's good news for environmentalists and good reason to get over our bug phobia. Simply put, those looking for an alternative source of protein to incorporate into their everyday eating habits should seriously consider things that crawl and fly. As New York City-based developer of cricket flour protein bars EXO Protein (see also page 84) points out, "Are crickets vegan or vegetarian? Technically no. But depending on your motivations for being vegan or vegetarian, you might be willing to eat insects."

Some of the high-tech, edible creations of ChefJet Pro.

Athletes have already embraced powdered forms of insects as a protein shake replacement; good for building muscle and delivering energy to the body in its most fundamental and easy-to-digest form. But what about the rest of us, who are neither thrilled by the idea of eating insects nor entirely against it? Well, restaurants and food trucks are upping the ante, responding to this ambivalence by putting bug-based dishes on their menus that are actually appealing enough to take a chance on. Washington, D.C.'s Oyamel Cocina Mexicana has had *chapitos* — a Mexican cricket taco — on the menu for years. Welsh restaurant Grub Kitchen attempts to win converts by making bugs a normal part of a meal, partnering with The Bug Farm, where the restaurant's crucial ingredients are raised sustainably. Don Bugito, a San Francisco food truck playfully labeling itself a "Prehistoric Snackeria," has embraced the weirdness of eating bugs wholeheartedly, developing a colorful, childlike bug logo and pasting cartoon sunglasses onto its pictures of bugs on plates.

For those who might want to try their hand at growing their own food, Livin Studio, a collaborative design development company based in Austria, has created Farm 432,

a compact and self-contained laboratory for hatching, nourishing, and harvesting black soldier fly larvae, which the company explains, "are one of the most efficient protein converters in insects, containing up to 42% of protein (dried), a lot of calcium, and amino acids." If that sounds unappetizing, a few distressing facts about industrial animal production may be enough to turn you on to entomophagy. According to Livin Studio, "one third of croplands worldwide are used to produce animal feed, 80% of antibiotics are fed to animals, and livestock is the single biggest cause of climate change." In order to counter this, Livin Studios has created a futuristic product that could fit in your living room.

With the innovative Fungi Mutarium, Livin Studio also reminds us that there is another way to dispose of waste to our benefit: use it as a base for growing an entirely new kind of food. A terrarium-like growing vessel with a glass-dome for a lid houses a series of tiny spheres made of agar, a "seaweed based gelatin substitute [that] acts, mixed with starch and sugar, as a nutrient base for the fungi." UV-sterilized plastic waste is added to this, along with an injection of fungal spores, which eventually digest the plastic and take over each tiny biosphere entirely. The result is an edible creation that has actually made use of something that would otherwise occupy space in a landfill.

Another project that seems to have roots in science fiction is the U.K. startup Growing Underground, which has already garnered support from London mayor Boris Johnson through the London Leaders business startup program. The audacious project, which received nearly one million euros in funding, much of it through a Kickstarter campaign, uses abandoned bomb shelter tunnels from the Second World War to grow pea shoots, several varieties of radish, mustard, coriander, red amaranth, celery, parsley, and arugula for private and commercial use (Michelin-starred chef Michel Roux, Jr. is a partner, and plans to use the greens at his restaurant Le Gavroche).

Growing Underground grows microgreens and herbs in a zero energy environment in old WWII bomb shelter tunnels.

London, England

Growing Underground

*

ABOUT: *An innovative urban farm in disused World War II shelter tunnels in London. Its mission is to deliver fresh produce with zero effect on the environment via green energy.*

Woop Woop Ice Cream

*

ABOUT: *"We use liquid nitrogen to freeze our ice cream in front of your very eyes, instantly transforming ingredients into a superb ice cream with the smallest ice crystals imaginable."*

Woop Woop Ice Cream is frozen on the spot using liquid nitrogen.

How does it work? "Crops are grown in a sealed, clean-room environment with a bespoke ventilation system, advanced lighting, and a sophisticated irrigation system that enable the farm to produce crops at very low energy. The farm's mission is to deliver fresh produce with zero effect on the environment, and all energy is sourced from green suppliers." The company will not reveal the exact location of its tunnel, only hinting that it is "less than two miles as the crow flies from the heart of London," perhaps to avoid thrill-seeking interlopers from trying to get in on the fun. But if the pictures are anything to go by, a trip down this particular rabbit hole is like a cross between The Matrix and Breaking Bad, a post-apocalyptic vision inhabited by somewhat mad scientists quite at home in their underground realm. And the micro-greens? They look exactly as micro-greens should: fresh, crunchy, nutritious, and most importantly, green, even though they have come into contact with no natural light during the growing process.

Whereas projects like Edible Growth and Growing Underground make you think about

Edible Growth

*

ABOUT: *Edible growth is an example of a future food product that forms a bridge between new technologies and authentic practices of growing and breeding food.*

the future of food, Woop Woop Icecream, as evidenced by its name, deals instead with good, old-fashioned fun. The Berlin-based company employs liquid nitrogen — once confined to scientific laboratories and middle school experiments — to freeze its concoctions on the spot, thereby creating a highly creamy product with almost no ice crystals. Part of their appeal stems from their fresh natural ingredients and interesting flavors, but let's be honest here: there is nothing like the thrill of watching your ice cream explode into being in a cloud of vapor, and eating it seconds later, your momentary worry that it may still have the ability to freeze your tongue overcome by the sheer pleasure of a well-made dessert.

Making "smart- use of natural processes like fermentation and photosynthesis."

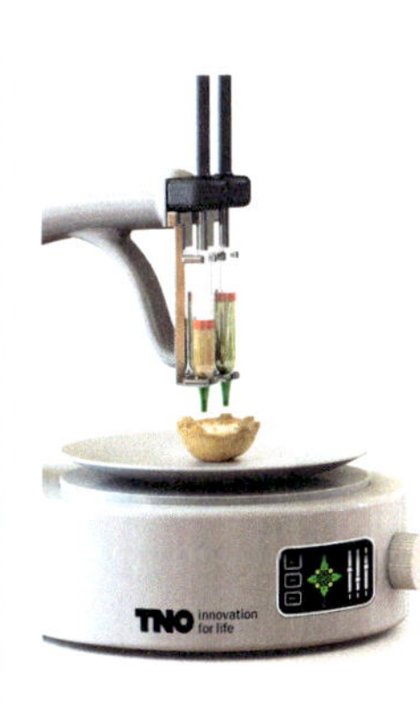

New Juice

Drink Your Fill

I t's a new trend with an old history, but this time around, something feels different. Up until now, health food has been a part of many alternative scenes, demanding that their adherents conform to certain rules for religious, spiritual or physical reasons. The twenty-first century has finally seen healthy food become a part of mainstream eating practices, and many new shops and companies are ready to light the way. Most of them eschew the esoteric décor of their predecessors in favor of smooth lines, light wood, and white interiors—perfect showcases for the clean, bright, and put-together lifestyles we crave. The bold graphics on custom glass bottles only serve to show off the naturally vibrant juice colors and broadcast their freshness. The goal is not to convince people to drink juice because it's healthy: it's to get them to drink juice because it's irresistible.

Daluma is the first company in Berlin to make eating healthy food—much of it raw, all of it organic—not only normal, but also downright delicious. It espouses

Daluma

*

ABOUT: *"We offer cold-pressed juices, superfood smoothies, a lot of raw food, and warm vegan dishes. Our approach is to make healthy living possible and easy for everybody."*

A bright, white, and clean atmosphere subliminally communicates the healthy outlook of the Berlin juice company Daluma.

a philosophy that has a lot to do with detoxing, nourishing, and energizing the body with the highest level of vitamins and minerals, buying only from organic and sustainable producers. Most of its juices are enriched with so-called superfoods — products like kale, açai, nettles, and chia seeds that pack a punch of energy and highly absorbable nutrients. These time-tested ingredients are revered as much for their nutritional properties as for the fact that many of them have been used in various indigenous cooking traditions going back to ancient times,

Tokyo, Japan

Why Juice?

*

ABOUT: *"Our nutritious juices
are easy and fast, yet surprisingly fresh.
Why Juice? uses a cold pressed juicer,
which crushes and presses fruits and
vegetables without destroying
enzymes and nutrients."*

proving their value through their staying power. Most importantly, however, the juices are cold-pressed through a high-pressure process, thereby preserving all their nutrients instead of destroying them through heating or pasteurization.

Why Juice? bases its philosophy on an old Japanese saying—*shun san shun shou*—meaning to grow and eat seasonally. The cold-pressed juice market is just heating up in Japan, and the hallmarks of a growing trend are all there: an interest in organic produce, healthy living and eating, and of course, companies like NON-GRID,

the creative studio responsible for executing the "Why Juice?" concept through beautiful design and attractive packaging. Their juices span the color and taste spectrum: deep purple beet mixed with apples and carrots, spicy lemon spiked with cayenne pepper, or dark green kale with cucumber and parsley. They can be bought individually or ordered in small, easy-to-drink packets as part of a detox program. They deliver in a cute tricycle wagon with a rough wooden crate at the front, thereby reinforcing their healthy, environmentally conscious image.

Nut milks are extracted in a similar process to juice, the nuts ground in a high-powered blender to produce liquid, and their nutritional benefits are also astonishing. Although the L.A. company Moon Juice also offers cold-pressed juices at its two shops, the real stars are their nut milks: creamy, rich concoctions made from sprouted nuts and seeds, often including mountain salt, honey, hemp, maca and stevia, as well as spices such as vanilla, cardamom, and ginger. Their website explains, "Moon Juice represents a holistic lifestyle that goes far beyond

Greene Street's signature glass packaging.
Brand design by Cassette.

Greene St. Juice Co.

*

ABOUT: *Cold pressed organic Australian produce combined with carefully selected superfoods and herbs to create functional, nutrient rich juice elixirs that are exquisite to taste and address whole body health.*

Director and co-founder Natalie Warner (above), and the brand's concept retail space designed by Travis Walton Architecture (left).

These juice makers market their products not just as refreshing drinks but as true magic potions.

juices, milks, and snacks. It's a healing force, an etheric potion, a cosmic beacon for those seeking out beauty, wellness, and longevity."

Based in Melbourne, a city at the forefront of food trends in Australia, Greene St. Juice Co. is actually named after a trendy street in Manhattan's SoHo neighborhood, where the two founders spent some time and hatched an idea. New York City can be a hard nut to crack, but they saw past the daily grind and instead encountered people who were using the energy of the city to fuel their dreams, not to get them down. Their juices are blatant references to the Big Apple, tinged with homesickness, hope, and

earnestness, and alongside the usual suspects appear a host of daring newcomers like dandelion, milk thistle, and ginkgo biloba leaf—all cold-pressed, raw, and organic, of course. These juice makers have all found success marketing their products not just as refreshing drinks or nutritional supplements, but rather as true magic potions, able to infuse drinkers with a certain special power—that of enjoying life to the fullest.

Tea not

Coffee,

Please

Oolong. Pu-erh. Matcha. Sencha. Just a decade ago, these words belonged to the realm of the well-studied academic; perhaps someone who spent years researching the traditional tea ceremonies of places like China, Japan, and Taiwan to write a treatise on them; an academic, not a bon vivant. Now, tea connoisseurship is reaching the mainstream. A ritual, seen as yet one more way to slow down and enjoy the small, beautiful moments in life, is gaining followers. The modern act of unwrapping a store-bought teabag, plopping it in a cup of already-cooling hot water, then drinking it without a thought is a far cry from the ritualized tea preparation processes of yore, which experts in Asia, like high priests communing spiritually with their drink, study for years to master. No longer consigned to the grandmas, tea is now fascinating a younger set, and these devotees are rejoicing in the details: the smooth, rounded teacups and clay vessels, the stream of infused water steaming from kettle to mug, the bittersweet, rich earthy taste of a tea　　»»»

with a particular *terroir* every bit as complex as a world-class wine.

For certain cultures where tea is grown, prized, and consumed on every important occasion, the tea ceremony can indeed feel almost akin to a religious ceremony: there are certain steps that must be done in the correct order, certain movements required to execute these steps perfectly, and certain objects—talismans almost, revered for their beauty and functionality—that must be used in a certain way. The result is something of a shrine to tea, and Adinda de Boer, a Dutch photographer living in Taipei, Taiwan and blogging under the name Wolves Table, captures this perfectly with her dark, mysterious, and quietly seductive photographs of the preparation of matcha—not a tea in the classic sense but rather a highly-prized,

For certain cultures where tea is grown and prized, tea preparation can almost feel like a religious ceremony.

Taipei, Taiwan
Wolves Table
ABOUT: "I'm a freelance photographer and stylist. I love to capture hidden treasures in daily life, like that one special moment that only lasts a second."

Studio Appétit

*

ABOUT: *Elixir is a world of potions that takes us back to different periods in human history, by evoking our subconscious memory of scents and flavours.*

Paper and Tea's bright, modern interior is the perfect place for an elegant tea ceremony.

Paper & Tea

*

ABOUT: *An elegant shop that celebrates the small, quiet ritual of tea preparation dating back centuries with high-quality tea leaves, beautiful ceramics, and paper goods.*

green tea powder with a vibrant color and flavor, and health benefits that reach almost mythical status.

Rather than being steeped in water as with tea leaves, matcha is stone-ground into a fine powder and then whisked into hot water to make a frothy green drink that can be much thicker and more flavorful than a traditional green tea. The ceremony also employs traditional ceramic bowls, which are used both to whisk the tea (with a light and delicate bamboo whisk called a *chasen*) and to drink it afterwards. Since matcha is time-consuming to

produce, it is much more expensive than other types of tea, and therefore must be served in a measured way and prepared with appreciation and restraint, sipped slowly, its grassy, bittersweet notes allowed to come to the fore. With careful and restrained food styling, low lighting, and earthy colors, de Boer evokes that quiet control that goes into preparing a cup of the highest quality tea in the world.

Paper & Tea not only also gets this devotion to quiet craft — they are also at the forefront of the tea-drinking movement. With their well-known slogan, ubiquitous on tote bags and posters around Berlin, "You Drink Coffee, I Drink Tea My Dear," they acknowledge the respect premium coffee has been given in the

past while assuring tea lovers that their drink of choice can be special too. We have got artisanal, fair trade coffee, they seem to say; why not single-origin, organic tea as well? The all-white interior of their Charlottenburg flagship store provides a serene and contemplative atmosphere—the most conducive to tea-drinking—and is also reminiscent of a gallery, with shelves displaying intricate stationery and ceramics of deep, rich colors from around the world. The space serves as both a conventional store and a learning center—where tea fanatics-to-be can come to learn the difference between a Yunnan Gold and a Shangri-La White. The block table in the center of the shop's main room is just for tea—an interactive ⟫⟫

We have artisanal, fair trade coffee; why not single-origin, organic tea as well?

ManuTeeFaktur

*

ABOUT: *Inspired by ancient tea growing and prepping methods discovered on world travels, this company makes and sells handmade tea from the best local ingredients.*

"While traveling off the beaten track, I discovered real tea."

display where each tea is given its proper due, with extensive sourcing information, pricing by weight, and of course, a petite petri dish full of leaves or buds, which you can sniff or "nose browse" to your heart's content.

In contrast to this quiet and contemplative image, ManuTeeFaktur presents tea as the product of adventure, inquisitiveness, and restless exploration. "While traveling off the beaten track," writes ManuTeeFaktur founder Manu Kumar, "through hidden tea rooms, vibrant night-markets, highland plantations, and nomadic tents I discovered real tea." Kumar's company is perhaps the intrepid rebel of the bunch, operating out of a courtyard building in Berlin's bustling and multi-cultural Kreuzberg neighborhood and offering contemporary products that are bold and colorful. Bottles of ManuTeeFaktur's cold Lemongrass or Tuareg Mint teas, with their bold graphics and promise of quick and healthy refreshment, have graced the café shelves in some of Berlin's trendiest neighborhoods, while jars of Kahwah Kashmiri Chai and India Masala Chai beckon tea drinkers with their large,

ManuTeeFaktur's handmade teas are imported from the very best sources around the world or grown just around the corner.

ManuTeeFaktur is perhaps the intrepid rebel of the bunch.

DSCHUNGEL MATE MIT FRUCHTSAFT
NATÜRLICH GESÜSST
TERERÉ
MATE
TEA
ManuTeeFaktur
"truly handmade"

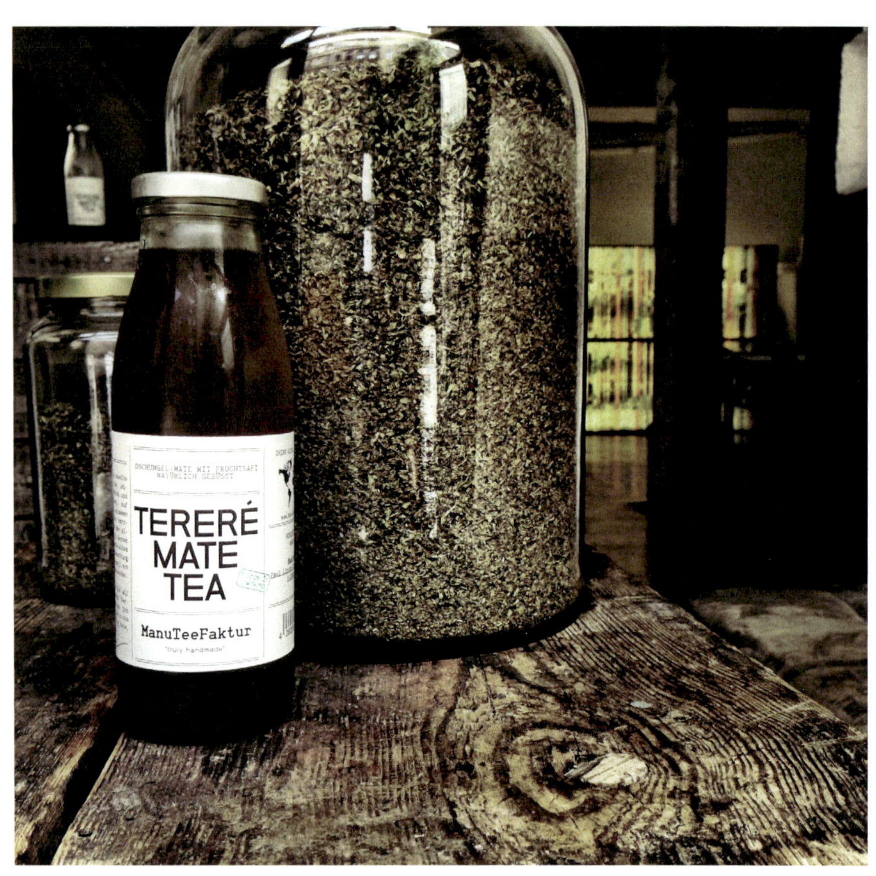

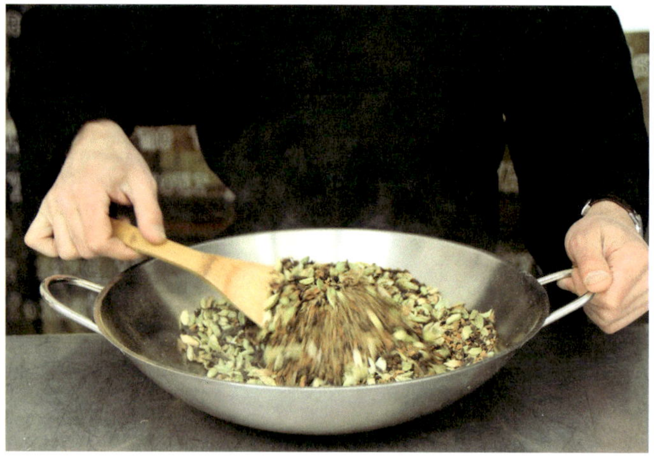

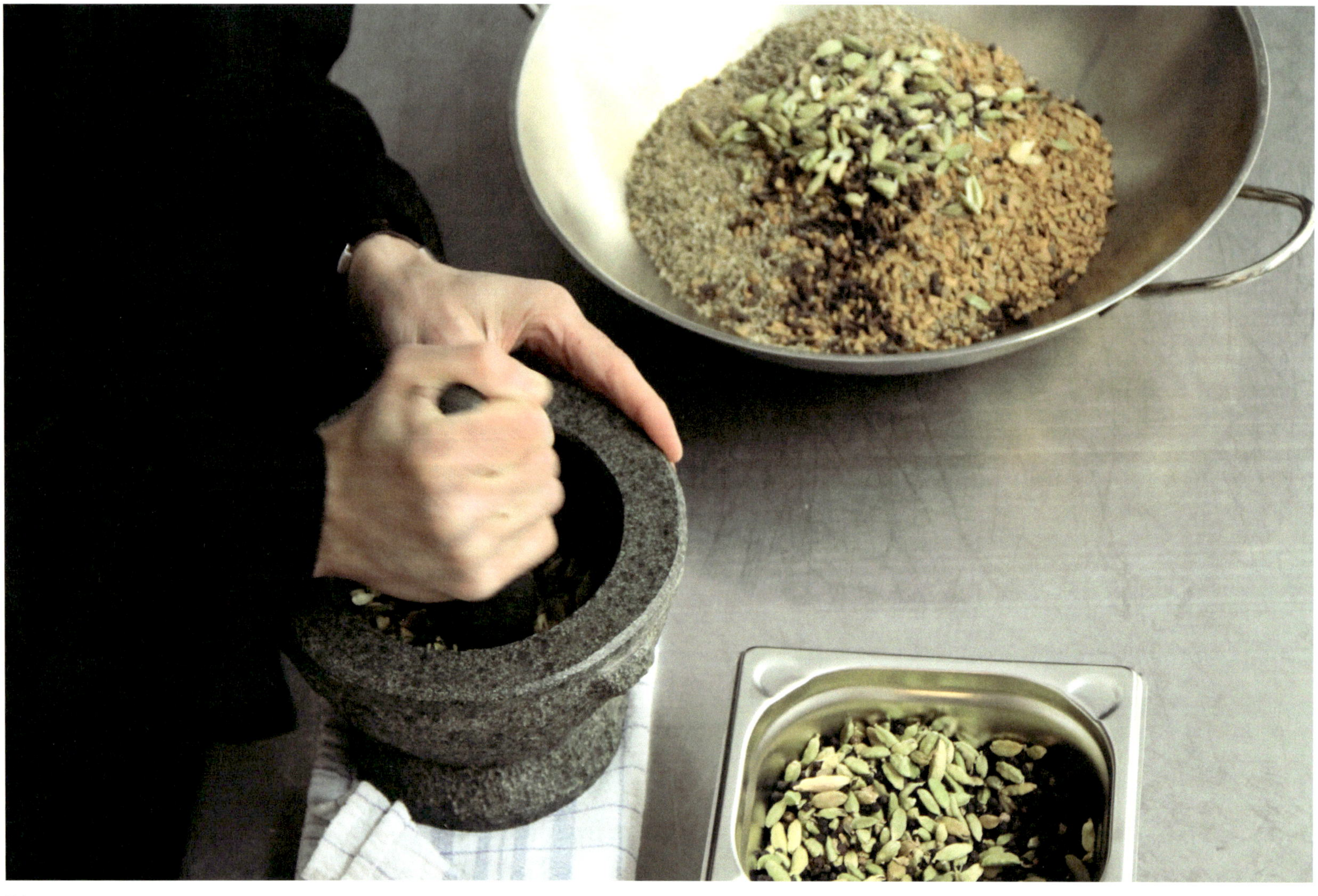

Brewing a cup of tea at ManuTeeFaktur's Kreuzberg shop and work space.

brightly colored leaves and labels. Whereas most tea companies seem to remain a bit mute on the personalities behind them, perhaps preferring to let the tea's own personality do the talking, ManuTeeFaktur is very much a labor of love; a one-man operation with Kumar and his enthusiasm for tea at the helm. This is local tea with a local personality; no need to go all the way to Japan to experience it. ▓▓▓▓

Tea as the product of adventure, inquisitiveness, and restless exploration.

The multi-step process of growing, harvesting, drying, and brewing that goes into a single bottle of ManuTeeFaktur tea.

"Teas are not only hand-mixed, they are hand-stamped as well."

Raising the Bars

Compact, *High-Energy* Delivery!

Sometimes you just want to deliver nutrients to your bloodstream as quickly as possible — no tableware and glasses, no formalities, none of the trappings of a typical, sit-down meal. What started with hardcore athletes eager to pack their bodies full of energy has now gone mainstream. New companies are updating the traditional power bar with some pretty inventive, unusual, and occasionally downright bizarre ingredients. The results are thought provoking and delicious; a far cry from the energy bars of years past that were little more than nuts and syrupy sweetness covered in chocolate.

EXO (see also page 84) a New York-based startup using cricket flour to create high-protein power bars, proclaims that "crickets are the new kale" on its website. It uses athlete testimonials and photos of high-energy workouts to stir up interest for its products, which come in flavors like Cocoa Nut and Peanut Butter and Jelly. Its message is one of nourishing your body while doing minimal damage to the

Illustrated prairie and farm animals on Epic Provisions' bars are evocative of pioneer days.

environment. Epic Provisions takes another tack, making squares and bars from grass-fed meats like bison, beef, lamb, and turkey sourced directly from farmers and ranchers. These animals have spent their lives on the plains and prairies, eating what they have eaten for centuries, and making less of an impact on the environment than corn-fed cattle and barn-raised sheep. Epic's simple, off-white packaging with old-fashioned animal illustrations mirrors its vision: they are peddling twenty-first century pioneer bars.

The Berlin-based company Die Kraft des Urstromtals (The Force of the Glacial Valley) harnesses the romantic notion of a return to ancient eating practices to create vegetarian, vegan, and paleo energy bars with names like Sabre-Toothed Tiger (red deer jerky,

Austin, TX, USA

Epic Provisions

*

ABOUT: *Specializing in conveniently packed, meat-based protein snacks that are unique and flavor-forward, EPIC Provisions believes that epic foods should inspire epic health.*

Berlin, Germany

Die Kraft des Urstromtals

*

ABOUT: *Food without any flavour enhancers, made delicious with real ingredients. This is how we started making our own high-energy snacks.*

Die Kraft des Urstromtals make daring vegetarian, vegan, and paleo energy bars with unusual ingredients.

What started with hardcore athletes eager to pack their bodies full of energy has now gone mainstream.

Berlin, Germany
Die Kraft des
Urstromtals

Exo Protein

*

ABOUT: *Exo makes nutrient-dense real food bars, designed by a three-Michelin-starred chef. The bars combine minimally-processed cricket flour protein with ultra-premium ingredients.*

garlic, and nuts), the Mandrill (almonds, chili, and lime juice), or the Honey Bear (fruits, nuts, and honey). Sure, our cave-dwelling ancestors would hardly have been able to compress their most nutritious foods into compact bars, but Die Kraft des Urstromtals offers a twenty-first century update of an ancient method of nourishment. Roo'bar, created by the owners of the first organic food Shop in Bulgaria, uses raw ingredients and superfoods like hemp and chia, baobab and ginger, or cranberry and maca to create natural, organic energy bars with no added sugar. All these products deliver a clear message: when pressed for time, it's far better to snack on densely nutritious food bars then to resort to a pack of chips or a fast food meal.

Mixing the raw ingredients to form organic bars by Bulgaria-based RooBar.

Sofia, Bulgaria

Roo'bar

*

ABOUT: *100% raw, organic bars with
only four to five ingredients, created by the team
behind the first organic shop in Bulgaria.*

I'll Drink

Spirited Spirits

to That

and Bold Beers

There was a time not too long ago when only wine-drinkers were taken seriously when it came to enjoying alcohol (and usually French wine drinkers at that). Wine, with its bouquets and *terroirs* and origin myths and fancy labels, was the only thing you could drink regularly and rave effusively about without being considered a louche layabout or worse, an alcoholic.

But now it's all changed, and much for the better. Beer is considered to be as varied, artisanal, and enjoyable as some of the world's best wines. There is a greater variety on the market, and what's more, serious beer lovers have been the impetus for creating a new global market, making it much easier to get specialty craft brews from San Francisco even when you're in Brussels, a great IPA from New York State even when you're in Copenhagen — or vice versa. Meanwhile, spirits lovers are going out of their way to obtain a rare whiskey from Taiwan instead of a Talisker, to seek out a clean, crisp juniper liqueur from Iceland over a Hennessey

Berlin, Germany

Preussische Spirituosen Manufaktur

*

ABOUT: *Reclaiming an over one hundred year old distillery in the Berlin neighorhood of Wedding to produce artisinal brandies, vodkas, and schnapps.*

It's about participating in DIY culture, while also chasing a dream.

gin, or to bag a strong, smoky Mexican mezcal over the more conventional tequila.

What is behind this urge to go for more specialized and creative versions of alcohol from smaller, more local companies? Well, part of it is the same tendency we are seeing in culinary trends worldwide: the search for authenticity, which, to many foodies, is the same thing as good taste. The notion that, in our globalized world, making more personal connections with products that come straight from their makers is a good step towards keeping things local. It's about participating in DIY culture while also chasing a dream: if we buy something directly from the person who made it, who, it turns out, is not so different from us, it's just a short step further to imagining we could somehow do it ourselves.

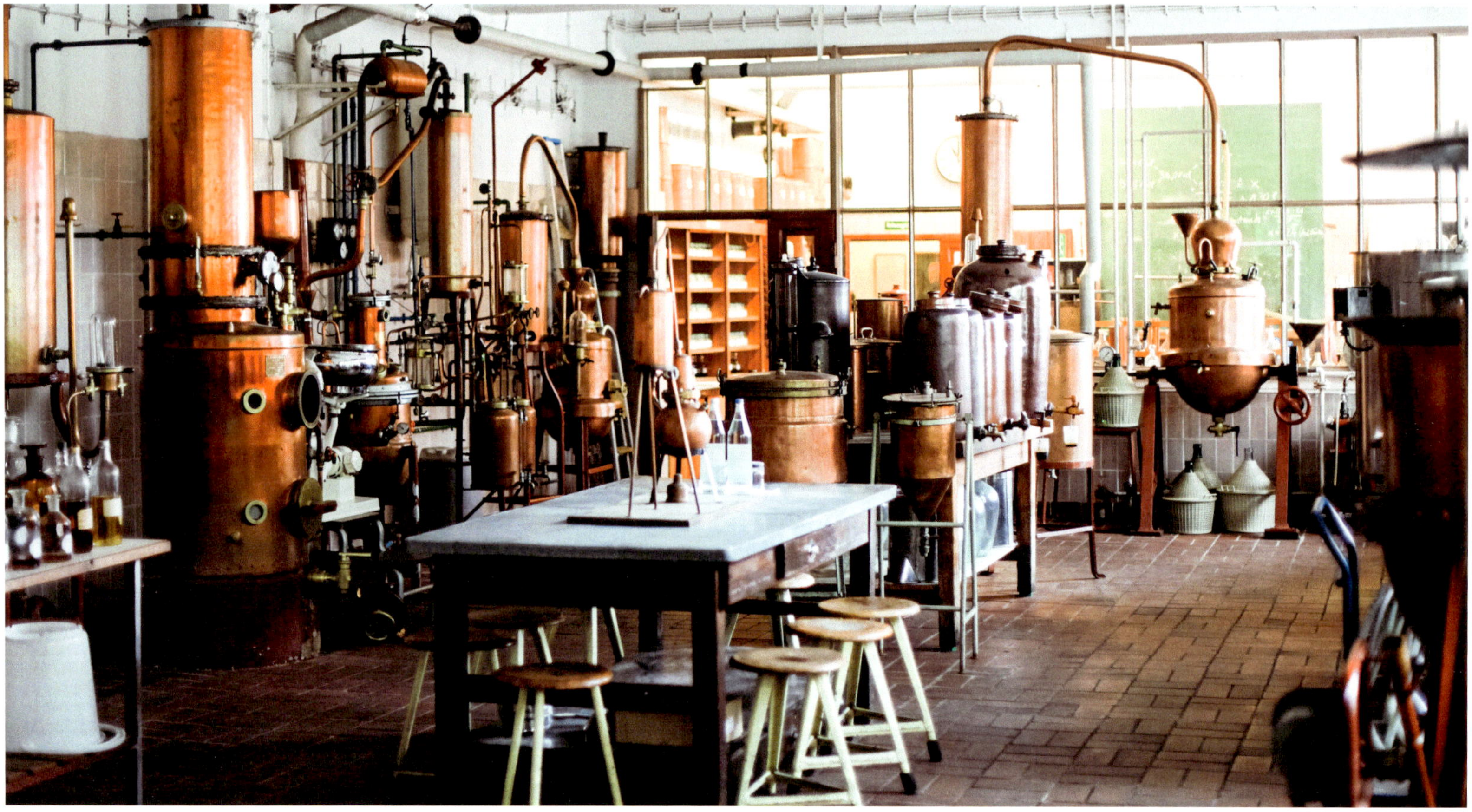

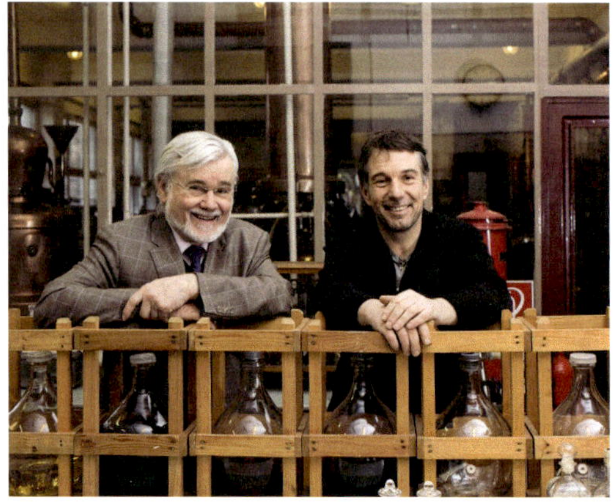

The distillation room is located inside a 100-year-old building in Berlin's Wedding neighborhood.

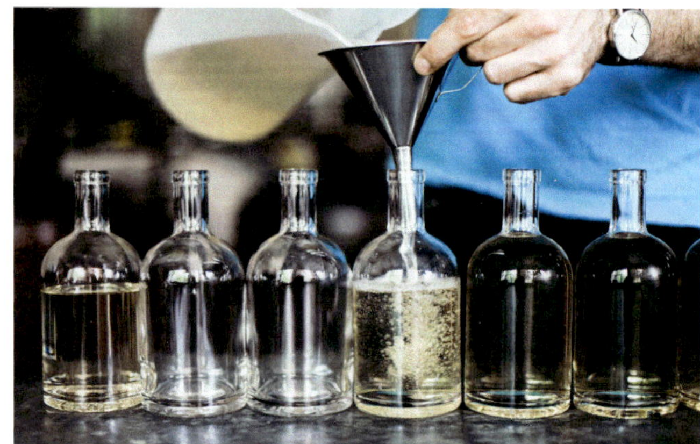

Drink Syndikat offers subscribers the chance to make two kinds of drinks each month: a classic, and a reinterpretation of it.

If we buy something directly from the person who made it, we can easily imagine doing it ourselves.

It's difficult to pinpoint where the craft beer trend started, although in the last five years or so it's really taken hold in the U.S., making a country that used to be infamous for its watered-down, flavorless excuses for beer into the reigning champion of exciting brews. Nowadays, you cannot open a bar or restaurant in New York or San Francisco and expect to stay open without offering a wide selection of craft beers on tap. You cannot be a self-respecting bartender in any major American city without knowing your Pale Ales from your India Pale Ales from your double and triple India Pale Ales. Like any trend, however, this one started with a few daring doers all over the world. Although we can't quite call it the beginning anymore, it may in fact be a new kind of beginning—one in which a more mature, measured, and educated love of alcoholic beverages is allowed to take hold of the mainstream, and there are people and places just as dedicated and knowledgeable working behind the scenes to make that happen.

Leading the way outside of America is Germany, a country whose strong tradition of beer brewing according to strict so-called "purity laws" might have actually kept out the craft brewers for good. Not so, explains

Berlin, Germany

Drink-Syndikat

*

ABOUT: *Drink-Syndikat presents a new box every month with handmade ingredients and recipes for six wondeful drinks, focusing on classics from the Roaring Twenties and modern variations.*

Erik, one of Drink-Syndikat's founding members, grew up in a family of wine and spirits sellers

Chase Distillery

*

ABOUT: *Twenty years' experience in potato farming led to the founding of the artisinal potato chip company Tyrell's; the same English farm is now producing small-batch, artisanal gin and vodka.*

Small-batch, hand-crafted alcohols are at the forefront of the cocktail revival.

Chase Distillery's gins and vodkas are made from produce grown on a small farm in the English countryside.

Klaas Twietmeyer, whose blog Hops Hysteria has been following and lauding the Teutonic beer fervor since 2012: "The fact that beer is getting special recognition in Germany at the moment and that the term 'craft beer' is on everyone's lips is hardly surprising, but rather long overdue. For far too long, beer here has been a cheap, boring drink that always taste the same and doesn't allow for much variety. The German Purity Law cannot entirely escape blame for this. But that means the growth of this new generation of self-made brewers is even more worth celebrating: they recognize that much more is possible."

Twietmeyer himself recognized that much more was possible, and went beyond the virtual realm in 2012 and 2015 to brew his own beer. Most recently, he has collaborated with other beer lovers to open the Beyond Beer shop in Hamburg; a place where beer lovers and skeptics alike can discover new brews and get their hands on old favorites. His trajectory and that of his blog demonstrates the DIY aesthetic in full: starting off as an admirer, he has become a participant in this ever-growing scene, and may offer products that turn other admirers into participants as well.

In Copenhagen, Mikkel Borg Bjergso of the craft beer brewery Mikkeller had a similar DIY-to-professional transformation: formerly a math and physics teacher with a passing interest in hops, he had the idea of mixing French press coffee with an oatmeal stout and the audacity to call it Beer Geek Breakfast, winning a competition in the process and jumpstarting his career in brewing. These days, his beer has reached as far as Chicago and Alaska, and is served at everything from neighborhood craft beer bars to Michelin starred restaurants, proving that the dream he states on his website,

Artisanal gins and vodkas, distilled to preserve
the flavors of the English countryside.

Hops Hysteria

*

ABOUT: *This German blog has taken up the task of reporting on modern beer culture in all its extraordinary facets, showing consumers just how unbelievably complex beer can be.*

to "make quality beers a serious alternative to wine and champagne when having gourmet food," has come true.

For those who also envision a career in hops and barley, but are not quite sure where to start, London product designer Freddie Paul presents a sleek, stylish conversation piece called the Beer Tree. There has certainly been a movement in recent years toward doing everything yourself, but cooking, baking, making jam, even making ice cream, are all fairly easy DIY food projects in comparison to the seemingly confounding act (well, if you've never done it before) of brewing beer. There are just too many steps, too many ingredients, and worst of all, far too much equipment for those of us who work normal jobs and live in somewhat normal houses and apartments to ever have enough time, space (bathtub brewing, anyone?) or know-how to make a batch of our very own beer. As he explains, "Traditional home-brew kits are ugly collections of plastic barrels and a mess of hoses, usually stored in

The Beyond Beer shop in Hamburg is a haven for beer enthusiasts.

London, England
Clapton Craft

*

ABOUT: *We are a craft beer and growler refill shop on Lower Clapton Road in Hackney. We sell a wide range of local, U.K. and imported beer in bottle, as well as … from eight rotating taps.*

a user's garage out of sight. Beer Tree aims to combat this problem by encompassing the entire beer brewing process in one single, elegant product."

Since the Beer Tree is constructed to direct the brewing process from top to bottom, it becomes a gravity-driven demonstration of how brewing works—one that could be mistaken for a piece of art installed in your living room. The five-step process is on view for all to see: treated water is heated to 80°C in the first tank, and then allowed to flow into the second, where grains of malt barley and wheat are mixed in, achieving a thick consistency called wort. This liquid is then transferred to the kettle and mixed with hops, then boiled for 60 to 90 minutes. After being cooled to 25°C, it is then transferred to the fermenter, where yeast is added to spark the process. The final product is ten liters of beer in ten days, but there is also a hidden result: the Beer Tree is not just

Mikkeller Brewery

*

ABOUT: *A microbrewery that aims to elevate beer to the level of wine and champagne — a worthy companion to gourmet food and an artisanal drink in its own right.*

an attractive object with a specialized functionality; it is also a starter kit for beer fanatics. Those who use the Beer Tree to make their first few bottles, and are able to see the miraculous process in front of them, may end up becoming the next generation of talented microbrewers.

The fascination with artisanal alcohol goes far beyond beer, however; in this new atmosphere of enthusiasm for all things alcoholic, sparkling wine and spirits are also getting their due. The founders of the Berlin-based Preussische Spirituosen Manufaktur ("Prussian Spirits Manufacturer") are reviving the spirits trade in more ways than one: not only are they distilling some of the best spirits in Germany from tried-and-true recipes, they've also taken over a 100-year-old brick factory space to do it in. Housed in the former workspace of the Prussian Research and Educational Center for the Fabrication of Spirits,

Mikkeller aims "to make quality beers a serious alternative to wine and champagne when having gourmet food."

Steps along the way: the brewing process at Copenhagen's Mikkeller.

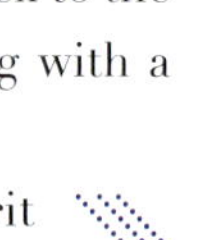

founded in 1874, the Preussische Spirituosen Manufaktur of today churns out bottles of Adler Gin and Vodka, an eagle artfully incorporated into its striking logo, and essences of Williams pear, raspberry, and sloe.

Chase Distillery was once a small potato farm in Herefordshire, England. Its owner, William Chase, first envisioned and successfully grew an artisanal potato chip business by the name Tyrells. After an auspicious trip to the U.S., Chase realized what he probably already knew: potatoes can become something delicious to drink as well. So began the next step in his career: Chase Distillery now sells artisanal gins, vodkas, and other specialty liqueurs, all distilled according to traditional methods to preserve the flavors of the English countryside. Thanks to companies like these, a true art form is capturing the attention of a new generation. Expertly crafted drinks that were once thought to sit squarely in the realm of the elderly — or at least the irretrievably square — are now seen as exciting representatives of a certain cultural moment once again.

In the past few years, loads of foodie startups have compiled and sent out food boxes, allowing those with little time but the urge to cook a real meal at home — especially creative urban professionals — to put together a dinner in a short time. Drink Syndikat, a Berlin-based startup, is now answering the question of what to do before that cooking session starts — when you have just gotten home from work and all you want is a good stiff (but of course artisanal, handcrafted, and delicious) drink. Hitching their wagon to the gourmet box trend, Drink Syndikat makes it easy for drinks enthusiasts to find out about mixing cocktails by creating a sort of "spirits CSA box" for the alcoholically inclined. Each month, their box contains enough supplies to make six drinks of two different types: one that harks back to the Prohibition-era Roaring Twenties, along with a contemporary recreation of it.

Each box showcases one type of spirit (along with a handy written history of its

Sampling artisinal alcohol: a well-made schnapps will have a complex bouquet, just like wine.

Beer Tree is everything you need to make beer in one eye-catching sculpture.

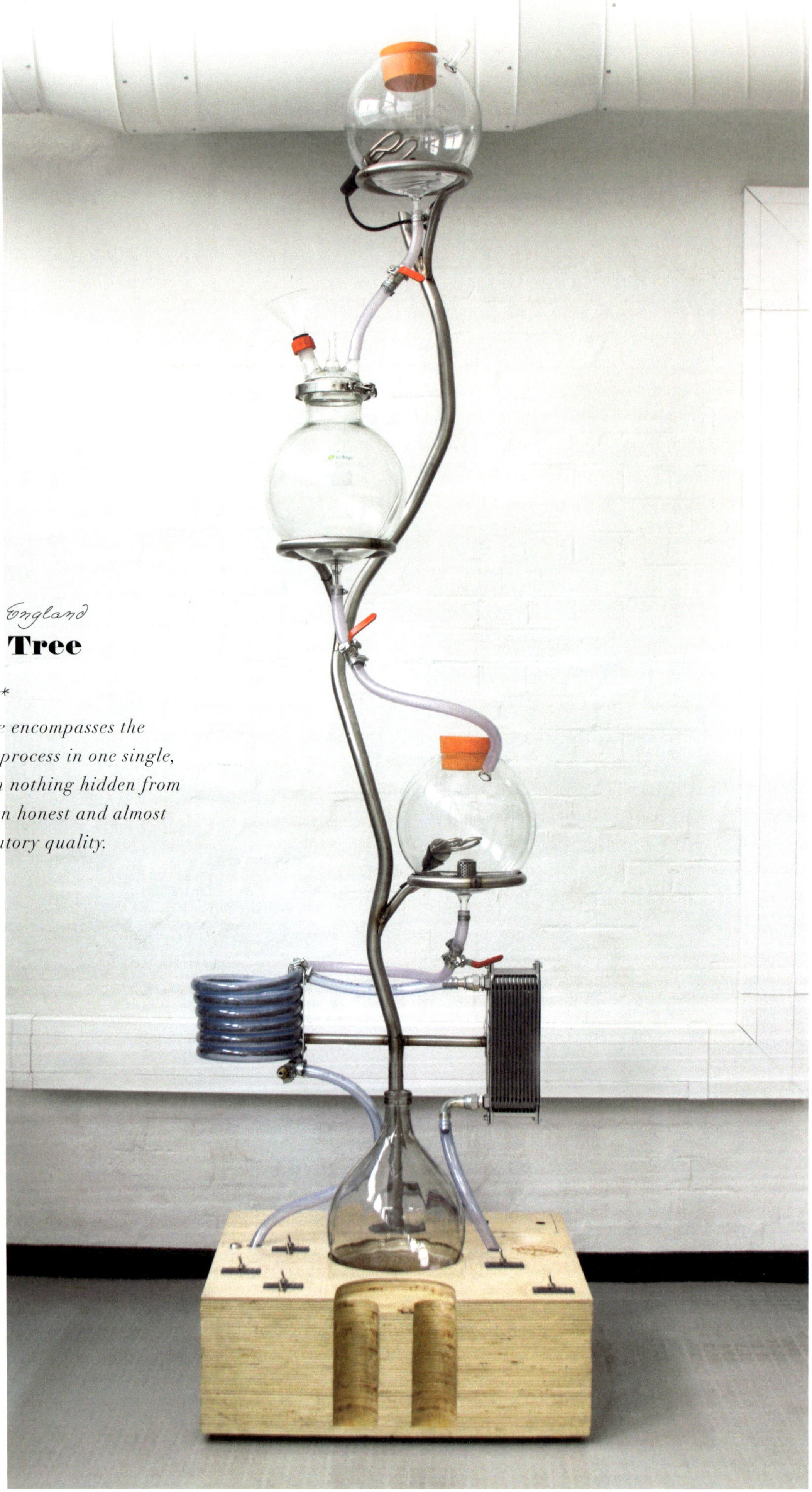

invention, development and importance within society). Spirits are mostly sourced locally (within Germany) from small companies that care about taste, quality, and remaining true to a long-held tradition. The small, numbered bottles hark back to the era of the apothecary – the true mixologists of another age – and subtly direct the user as to the order in which the drinks should be mixed, while the vintage lettering and central graphic on each box draw the eye and bring the mind around to a time when enjoying cocktails was not only a stylish pastime but a potentially dangerous political statement.

In another bid to reintroduce people to traditional booze, the mobile Sektgar traverses Berlin serving German sparkling wine to the people (*sekt*, much like the Italian *prosecco*, means "sparkling wine" in German). A few years ago, founder Edgar Gerold was surprised to find that, although food-lovers were becoming more and more

London, England

Beer Tree

*

ABOUT: *Beer Tree encompasses the entire beer brewing process in one single, elegant product, with nothing hidden from the user, giving it an honest and almost self-explanatory quality.*

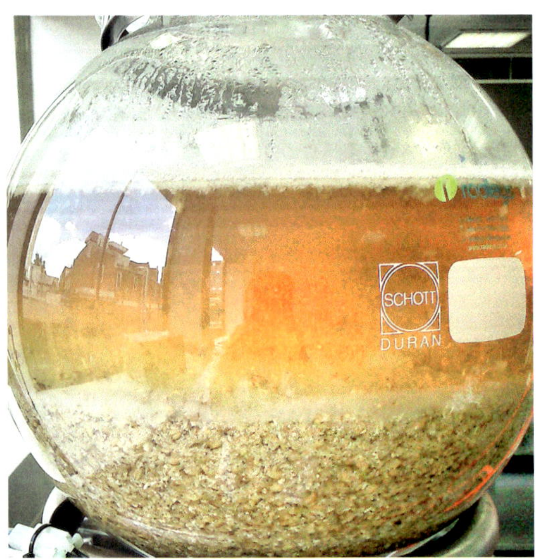

obsessed with small, handmade offerings from local producers, they were all too likely to stick with the big, mainstream brands when it came to sparkling wine. Some of the best vineyards in the world are in Germany, and some of the best vintners also like to make some bubbly along with their wines. So called *Winzersekt*—sparkling wine from local producers handcrafted in limited quantities each year—is what Sektgar peddles with a combination of charm, style, taste, and innovation—yet one more foot soldier in the fight against the corporatization and globalization of food and drink.

Berlin, Germany

Sektgar

*

ABOUT: *A mobile bar in Berlin selling mainly German sparkling wines from small vineyards. The aim: to show how many fabulous sparkling wines are out there, all crafted with passion.*

Introducing the world to some of the best small vineyards producing sparkling wine in Germany.

Tasty Treats,
Moveable
by Land
Feasts
or by Sea

No one ever said a good meal had to be enjoyed sitting down. Indeed, some of the best meals and most authentic delicacies all over the world are best enjoyed standing up, on the go, or at least sitting at a rickety stool in front of a makeshift kitchen at an outdoor market. Who has not experienced the intense pleasure and childlike joy of walking leisurely down the street while licking an ice cream cone? In New York City, the street culture is very much based on the idea of quick snacks—a slice of pizza folded in half and eaten while walking, a hotdog consumed in a rush, the classic blue-and-white Greek coffee shop to-go cup with "we are happy to serve you" emblazoned on the side, spelled out in coffee steam. In many parts of Central and South America, China and Southeast Asia, those who prepare food on the street represent centuries of tradition, and are revered every bit as much as indoor restaurant chefs.

These days, as the location of a meal becomes just as important as the meal itself, amateur and professional 

Sandwiches
Burgers
Seasonal food
On the road
Sweet Rolls
Aloha
CARAVAN MADE
Built in 1970
SANDWICHES
GINGER PORK
BOU BOU
SWEET POTATO
VEGGIE BURGER
6€
KIPS DE YUCA 1.5€

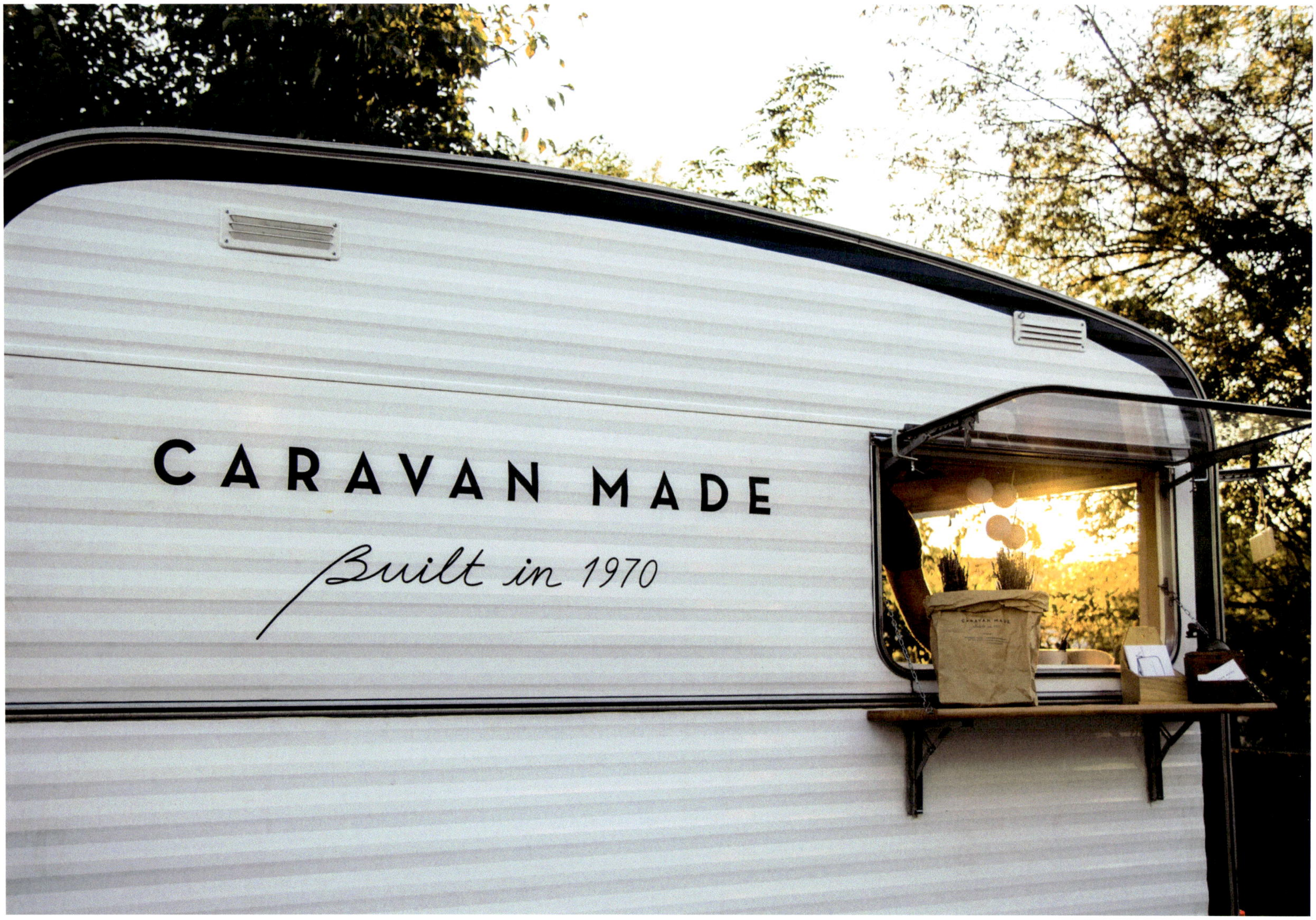

The new food to go: inventive meals made with local ingredients and served from street food trucks.

No need to invest in a brick-and-mortar space.

chefs are moving their feasts from the restaurant setting to private dining rooms, home kitchens, parks and gardens, rooftops, and streets. Secret supper clubs were a culinary highlight over the last decade, as patrons got a thrill from going somewhere unconventional and being served in a place where restaurants technically weren't allowed. The western hemisphere has caught onto the street food trend, and markets have popped up all over America and Europe, offering international cooks and bakers the opportunity to showcase their wares. No need to invest in a brick-and-mortar space; a street food stall can offer customers a low-cost, low-commitment way to taste new and unusual delicacies. Nowadays, visiting a street food market tops the list of weekend or vacation activities for many young and inquisitive people: an easy way to experience a new culinary culture and interact with locals, it is viewed as an exciting new form of entertainment and culture "sampling" on par with clubbing, bar-hopping, museum-going, or a visit to a flea market.

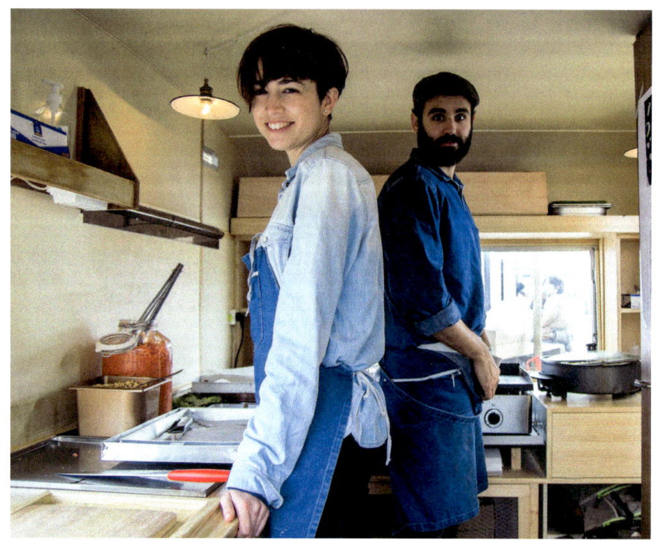

One of Caravan Made's delectable
sandwiches.

Barcelona, Spain

Caravan Made

*

ABOUT: *"We wanted to create a casual
and approachable gastronomic project.
And with a kitchen 'on wheels,' we saw
a way to get close to people."*

Part of the thrill of the food truck is the thrill of
the chase—if your favorite lunchtime spot is always on the move and always coming up with new
recipes, you're never quite sure what you're going
to get. But sometimes, this just makes the bond
stronger—you know that whatever you are eating
has been made by the person who is handing it to
you; no middlemen, no secrets. You can probably
also ask where the ingredients are from, whether
they were sourced just this morning, and what
might be next on the menu. The personal trumps
the reliable, the new and exciting is much better
than the known and the routine.

Melding all these properties is Caravan
Made, a quaint little food truck operating out of
Barcelona and the passion project of Spanish
couple Silvia Cabra and Javi Ruz. While
Barcelona has always had a vibrant food culture,
recent years have seen young people moving
away from traditional restaurants and bars and
turning instead towards the surprising and unconventional: weekly open-air markets, pop-up
restaurants, and food trucks dot the landscape,
and Caravan Made is just one thriving
part of this.

Caravan Made specializes in fresh sandwiches of all sorts — of little interest to Americans and Brits but somehow more difficult to find in many European countries. Ingredients have been sourced at seaside markets outside Barcelona early in the morning, their bread is unquestionably organic. Their vintage caravan, somehow fittingly, was discovered in Berlin and then refurbished. Many of these places use food trucks to try out concepts and gain a following in preparation for opening a real restaurant, but Silvia and Javi seem content with what they have, the freedom of movement and scheduling it brings them, and the way it brings them closer to their customers and to other people in Barcelona doing interesting things with food. As it turns out, food trucks can become a social as well as a culinary movement, and that's the best part about them.

Atelier Culinário

*

ABOUT: *Atelier Culinário is the home of a well-traveled and cosmopolitan artist, Sabine Hueck, to whom cooking is an art, among many other things related to the world of gastronomy.*

Also in Barcelona is Rooftop Smokehouse, a self-proclaimed experimental kitchen combining many elements that make outdoor dining so appealing: a roving, makeshift kitchen full of enthusiastic experimenters, ready to combine old-fashioned, time-tested elements of food preparation (smoking, brewing, and pickling, for instance) and take them anywhere, showing up at street food markets and pop-up events, conducting workshops, and catering

Sabine Hueck takes inspiration from around the world,
including her German and Brazilian backgrounds and many
other places where she has lived

Atelier Culinário is all about enjoying good food with good (and hungry) friends.

private parties. They built a smoker out of an old wine barrel, source ingredients at short notice from wherever they are — everything from beef, pork, and duck to octopus and mussels — and tailor their events to their audiences. This kind of theatricality has always been a part of the dining out experience. Only now, chefs are taking it out of the conventional restaurant setting, wowing diners with their ability not only to be creative, but also to do it all spontaneously. What is more, Rooftop Smokehouse presents itself as a collection of friends inspired to do something together, and that is their greatest appeal: watching them work and tasting their

Barcelona, Spain

Rooftop Smokehouse

*

ABOUT: *"An experimental makeshift kitchen,
we work on brewing our own beer, pickling, smoking,
and fermenting. We are rediscovering old techniques
and implement them via pop-up restaurants."*

Rigging up the homemade smoker to produce expertly smoked meat and fish.

creations, you want to be invited into their world to become a part of their merry band of smokers, if only for the length of a single meal.

Up north in the capital of Finland, Streat Helsinki shows what it's like to establish a street food market as an entirely new element of a city's personality — especially when the temperature is very often freezing cold. What does it take to set one up, spread the word, and get

people excited? In the organizers' own words: "A fleet of six food trucks touring the suburbs, a nighttime feast featuring five food kiosks, eleven workshops with 40 moderators, and a street food festival starring 66 street food entrepreneurs attracting over 30,000 street food lovers and selling close to 55,000 portions." It is a testament to just how important the street food phenomenon has become that the heads of Streat

Helsinki and other street food festivals like it see themselves as not just event organizers but also purveyors of a certain cultural message and representatives of their city, creating something that will be an important element in attracting new visitors.

In New York City, Chefs Club presents a high-end version of a moveable feast. Curated each year by renowned culinary magazine *Food & Wine*, the intimate dinners offer a small number of guests exclusive access to chefs who have won the magazine's prestigious Best New Chef award. Chefs create tasting menus of their signature dishes and present them personally. Here we see the idea of the private supper club or pop-up dinner coming full circle: was once was conceived as a way for not-really-professional chefs to cook in the not-quite-legal kitchens of their own homes, a low hassle way to bond with diners and try out new dishes, has now been adopted by those on the highest rungs of the restaurant industry once again, enticing diners with a personal connection to chefs and their creations. In turn, these chefs have been vetted by a magazine that prides itself on identifying the best. So rather than walking into an unknown kitchen in a private apartment, ▶▶▶

Fish coming out of the homemade smoker, which was made out of a French wine barrel.

A sampling of treats from Rooftop Smokehouse.

Streat Helsinki

*

ABOUT: *Exploring street food as a phenomenon through various perspectives, with over 100 street food entrepreneurs sharing ideas and practices on a Finnish and international level.*

Streat Helsinki street food market sets up in one of the world's coldest capitals—and succeeds.

diners can enjoy a feeling of intimacy and secrecy while resting assured that the food will no doubt be spectacular.

In Berlin, Sabine Hueck's charmingly eclectic atelier presents a loving jumble of pots, pans, cooking tools, foods, and colorful décor one imagines comes from years of traveling the world. The informal but beautiful space matches Sabine herself, a chef and caterer born in Brazil but with German roots, her diverse cooking skills and passions built on time spent in Peru, Thailand, Mexico, Vietnam, France, and Portugal. The casual style of her business endeavors also mirrors the laid-back ethos of Berlin itself—a city that has been giving international, creative people the time and space to follow their own interests for years. And because she has both European and South American influences, a visit to her cooking space is just as likely to result in an impromptu sampling of ceviche as it is to lead to an international menu made with local Berlin and Brandenburg products. For some cooking classes, she even takes guests over to the nearby market on Winterfeldtplatz—one of the best weekly food markets in town—and teaches them what to look for, how to appraise

The heads of Streat Helsinki see themselves as purveyors of a cultural message.

PRAISE THE DOG
PRAISE THE DOG

RUOKA
TÄSTÄ

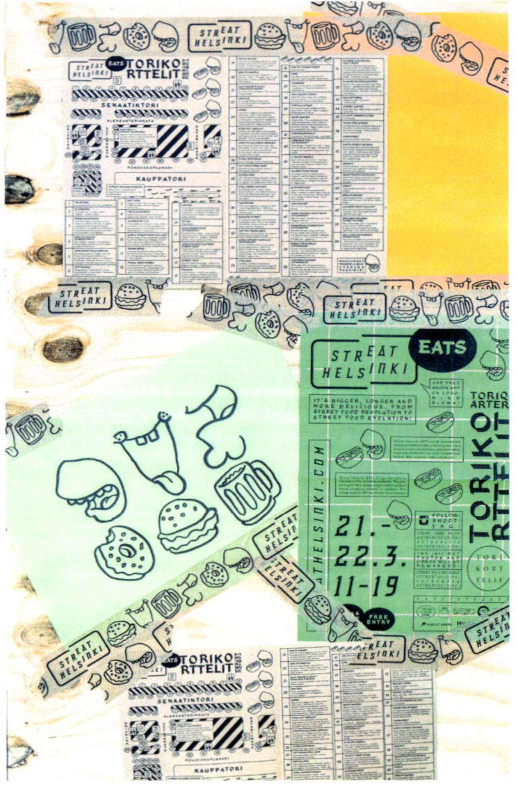

Establishing a street food market in a city that is often freezing cold.

STREET
VEGE
17.

PIZZA

It makes so much sense, you have to wonder why no one thought of it earlier.

Pizza delivered straight to the beach, courtesy of Pizza Pi.

US Virgin Islands

Pizza Pi

*

ABOUT: *Bringing the popular stateside food truck trend to the waters of the Virgin Islands in the form of a unique takeout experience that reflects the funky vibe of the islands.*

ingredients, and how to locate and identify the freshest, most seasonal produce for sale. This is a new vision of a cooking and catering company that takes it beyond business: a visit to Sabine's Atelier Culinário feels like a visit to a knowledgeable friend's house, even if it's your first time there.

And finally, ending as perhaps all things should, with a pizza. Except in this case, the pizza has been baked on a boat, and is delivered to you as you lie on the soft, white-sand beaches of the U.S. Virgin Islands. A pizza boat. It's never been done before, yet it makes so much sense, you have to wonder why no one thought of it earlier.

As the two founders of this remarkable project tell it, "PiZZA Pi brings the popular stateside phenomenon of food trucks to the waters of the Virgin Islands in the form of a family-friendly and unique takeout dining experience that also reflects the funky vibe of the islands." Made from a refurbished, 37-foot-long

A team led by award-winnig Nashville chef Erik Anderson and Alain Ducasse alum Didier Elena gets cooking. Right: A chunk of salt hangs above the dining area, like an altar to one of the world's most crucial ingredients.

boat that had been abandoned in Antigua for more than a decade, "Pi" anchors in Christmas Cove on Great St. James Island during the day, ready to whip up a New York-style or specialty pizza pie for anyone who might miss one, while also catering private events in the evenings. It brings a whole new meaning to pizza delivery, and since it's a never-before-seen, impromptu project, it means "they get to make up the rules as they go." Luckily, that's what moveable feasts are all about.

Chefs Club

*

ABOUT: *"Our mission is to showcase extraordinary signature dishes from the most talented chefs in the world, focusing on the winners of Food & Wine's prestigious Best New Chefs award."*

Prolific chef Linton Hopkins directs his team.

hefs Club offers diners the chance to sample dishes from acclaimed chefs around the world without booking a plane ticket. Staged in New York City's landmark Puck Building in the NoLIta neighborhood, the creative restaurant concept is actually a new version of an idea that originated in Aspen, Colorado. _Food & Wine_ magazine chooses four featured chefs each year from its list of Best New Chef award winners, showcasing their dishes on the menu and inviting them for personal events and masterclasses.

The Studio: alongside the innovative, chef-led menu, also plays host to visiting master chefs in the studio, these culinary artists push their creative boundaries while letting anexclusive audience into their world. Top and right page: Linton Hopkins Chefs Club Studio Dinner.

A dish by James Beard award winner Linton Hopkins.

Food & Wine Magazine chooses four featured chefs each year from its list of Best New Chef award winners.

MAINE DIVER SCALLOPS
Raw & Cooked
POTATO
SQUAB LIVER BONBON
WHITE TRUFFLE PORRIDGE
Danish Rye Bread, Goat Butter, Hickory Nuts, Tonka Beans
TART
Potato, Black Truffle
PIKE
Onions, Roasted Chicken Skin Bouillon, Preserved Lemon
ROASTED PIGEON
Cranberry, Juniper, Chestnut, Turnip, and Pine
HAY CUSTARD
Roasted Sweet Grass Hay, Fresh Cream, Barrel-Aged Maple Syrup
BURNT SUGAR & ROSEMARY PUDDING
Buttermilk Ice Cream, Pecan Sablé
MENU
1-10-15
ERIK ANDERSON
CHEF SESSIONS

Chef Erik Anderson of Nashville's Catbird Seat and Chicago's Intro is one of many chefs at the helm of pop-up dinners.

Innovative and contemporary dishes showcase the best award-winning chefs have to offer.

Chef Erik preparing dessert.

Left page: Michelin-starred French chef Gilles Epié works with Chefs Club executive chef Didier Elena.

A scallop and truffel dish by Gilles Epié.

Tempting diners with a personal connection to chefs and their creations.

Chef Hélène Darroze prepares her
menu for Chefs Club Studio Dinner.

Staging Food

Come Inside, Look Around, and Have a Bite to Eat

R are is the restaurant that subsists on food alone. If you have ever walked past a place on a warm summer evening, and felt beckoned by the buzz of patrons, the clink of wine glasses, the flicker of candles, and the soft sizzle of the grill, you've fallen pray to the lure of ambiance. You stop, gaze inside longingly, then walk in, perhaps not even bothering to look at the menu because it just feels right. You have found what you were looking for: a place to leave normal life behind, enter someone else's vision, and feel like you have become a part of something special.

Competing for attention, good reviews, and hard-earned cash, restaurants are upping their game from the inside out. Going out to eat is no longer just about choosing a table, picking a dish, and waiting for it to arrive. Nowadays, restaurants are striving to make eating out a comprehensive experience, a *Gesamtkunstwerk*, to take a page from Wagner. An upscale spot could have hired an entire design team to

Fontana di Trevi

Chef Benni Bräuniger

Lavanderia Vecchia

*

ABOUT: *An old laundrette turned hidden eatery, with a set menu of Italian classics. Vintage napkins, dishtowels, and aprons flutter on clotheslines — traces of the space's previous life.*

be responsible for its interior concept, ready to upholster the banquettes in matching textiles, source the finest dishware from a 100-year-old ceramic company in France, and have the most intricate glass chandeliers custom cut for each room, while a restaurant with a more cozy, old-fashioned vibe might go for mismatched flea market furniture, drinks in Weck jars, Edison lightbulbs, and exposed brick. Restaurants are thinking about, adjusting, and redesigning their image even when pretending they're not; it is just part of the deal these days when it comes to making a splash in the oversaturated restaurant market: being noticed, staying known.

Shops are getting in on the game too, with interiors that paint a fantastical 

dóttir

*

ABOUT: *Of Icelandic, Danish and Swedish heritage, the young chef Victoria Eliasdóttir sought inspiration in her Scandinavian roots for the culinary concept of dóttir.*

picture, humorously referencing what is for sale while inviting customers to linger. Shanghai-based creative studio Linehouse Design made quite an impression with two interiors for two very different shops: Lone Ranger, a hot dog shop next to the Hangpo river in Shanghai, was given a Wild West theme, including white painted shutters that open and close to reveal windows, and a geometric arrow pattern that wraps around the interior and across the tiled floor. Over a bright yellow ceiling stretches an intricate web of string lights, while wooden counters feature box cubbies and posts with hooks for hanging your hat. The overall effect is that of a playful but entirely modern homage to the old western saloon — even if such a thing only ever existed in our imaginations.

Little Catch updates the neighborhood fishmonger for a new generation, enticing

The interior of dóttir restaurant is airy, industrial, DIY, and so very Berlin.

Reds True BBQ

*

ABOUT: *Neon-lit religious imagery, metal caging, a maze of separate rooms within multiple levels, and old-fashioned, dark-wood details evoke an atmospheric mix of church and carnival.*

a younger crowd with a flashy neon sign and a cute, compact selling space. Fish are separated into deep metal troughs that customers can look through, while the catches of the day are spelled out with black lettering against a white background. Wooden shelves above provide space for cookbooks and other sundries. The floor-to-ceiling windows beckon shoppers inside, while providing enough display space for products like chilled white wines and sauces that go well with fish. The space feels clean, airy, and fun — quite in contrast to the chaotic, messy, and quite smelly traditional fishmongers you may have avoided in the past.

In Fukuoka, Japan, the design firm Movedesign reimagined an old wooden house in a residential neighborhood as an unconventional bakery, Boulangerie Kaiti. Its glowing checkerboard wooden floors are offset by light gray-blue walls and its central wooden table serves as a high-end display area for baked goods. A line of half-height windows lets in light

Paris, France

Clover

*

ABOUT: *Clover for good luck and happiness. Preparation and tasting takes place seamlessly, at what is, in the most literal sense, a dining room.*

Clover restaurant's interior, designed by Charlotte Biltgen, is the essence of flea market, vintage DIY, yet stylish and still very Parisian.

from the outside while preserving a sensation of privacy within a rarified realm, while a small vestibule acts as a transitional space between street and interior, giving customers the feeling of being welcomed into a private home.

Schemata Architects had a similar revival in mind when they designed Okomeya — a rice shop on the sleepy Miyamae shopping street in Tokyo. Run by Owan Inc., whose mission is to resolve issues in our daily living environment, the shop aims to revive the street by becoming a focal point of neighborhood activity, instead of letting it decline into a so-called "shutter street," where the buildings still stand but there is no sign of commercial life. Simple and modest, it has been set in a renovated wooden building that was once a vegetable shop.

At the other end of the Pacific Ocean and the other end of the design spectrum, L.A.'s Milk Jar Cookies evokes carefree childhood with its bright white interior, worn wooden display case, and triangle flags spelling out "Life is Short, Eat Cookies." A series of antique, flowery plates hanging on the walls and worn, vintage milk jugs hint at the ritual and tradition that go into this simple treat: just as preparing a cocktail or drinking a certain kind of coffee can make one feel like a sophisticated adult, there is nothing like eating a cookie with a glass of milk to make you feel like a kid again.

Exterior of the tiny Shanghai shop which design studio Linehouse transformed into Little Catch fishmonger.

Little Catch by Linehouse Design.

Shanghai, China

Little Catch

*

ABOUT: *An update of the neighborhood fishmonger sourcing and providing delicious, quality, and safe seafood to the Shanghai community.*

Lone Ranger

ABOUT: *A hot dog shop incorporating a wild west theme, Long Ranger features a playful composition of white weatherboards, raw timber, and custom print tiles with an arrowhead motif.*

Lone Ranger's playful, indie interior by Linehouse Design is juxtaposed with Shanghai's futuristic skyline.

Brothers and ice cream parlor owners Ryan and Eric Berley must have had the same idea in mind when they took over Shane Confectionary, a candy shop in Philadelphia dating back to 1863: glass jars line the walls behind them, full of enticing, multicolored sweets, and with their bowties and plaid jackets, the two look like the singing candy man from the opening scene of the movie *Willy Wonka and the Chocolate Factory.*

Restaurants looking to communicate an idea or philosophy to customers — not simply to feed them — let their comprehensive interiors speak for them, often scouring flea markets and antique shops to get just the right feel, or reimagining the interior of a space that was once used for something very different. The Quality Chop House is a restaurant,

THE QUALITY CHOP HOUSE
90
FOOD SHOP &
BUTCHER
90
SHOP
FOOD SHOP &
BUTCHER

The Quality Chop House

*

ABOUT: *"Our produce is delivered daily from trusted suppliers. A light touch from the kitchen allows the excellent meat, seafood, and vegetables to shine at their seasonal best."*

private dining room, wine bar, butcher, and food shop in a 100-year-old Victorian townhouse in London. With its black-and-white checkered floors and dark-wood benches, tables, and details, it instantly evokes a classic British pub. Its high, pressed-tin ceilings and antique lamps give it an air of sophistication though as if the corner pub had graduated into something more modern and alluring. The attached butcher shop uses old English cuts and rare breeds, while produce to create the seasonal menus is shipped in from all over the U.K. This is more than just a place to eat; it is an homage to classic English tradition, a valiant attempt to preserve something historical and cherished.

The Quality Chop House is not just a restaurant and butcher; it's also a shop selling curated, gourmet products.

At Clover in Paris's Saint-Germain-des-Prés neighborhood, designer Charlotte Biltgen has given restaurant-goers a new idea of what a Parisian eatery could look like; far from the dark, stuffy, staid establishments of yore, Clover is bright and airy, with unconventional design details that each has a story to tell. The two-tone wall consists of American shingles overlaid in a fishscale pattern, and a type of Japanese terracotta tile known as Raku, strategically cracked during firing for a kind of imperfect beauty the Japanese call wabi sabi. The parquet flooring was taken directly from freight trains of the SNCF, France's national railway. Most importantly, an open kitchen lets Michelin-starred chef Jean-François Piège and his

Fukuoka, Japan

Boulangerie Kaiti

*

ABOUT: *A bakery shop in an old, renovated Japanese house. The owner's philosophy: to offer delicious quality bread every day.*

assistants interact with guests, making the space feel more like a private dining room than a traditional commercial space in which servers and served are separated into two distinct realms. Nowadays, Biltgen's concept seems to say, it is not the chef who must please the customers, but the customers who must have the perceptiveness and good taste to truly understand and appreciate what the chef is trying to do.

In Berlin, two elegant restaurants have taken over raw spaces and transformed them while subtly hinting at what they were before. Lavanderia Vecchia Italian for "old launderette" does this with the strategic hanging of vintage embroidered textiles: napkins, tablecloths, aprons, and pinafores. The open-plan, industrial space in a back courtyard actually was a launderette before it became the city's worst-kept secret: a trendy, hidden Italian restaurant with a set menu of seemingly endless Italian dishes, including wine. The décor somehow reinforces the feeling of exclusivity and mystery: patrons enjoying a meal at one table may be half-hidden from their neighbors by a concrete column or exquisite embroidery. Pieces of starched white cloth flutter like light summer curtains as the dining rooms fill with the low buzz of conversation and the clash of pans from the open kitchen.

An old wooden house in a residential neighborhood reimagined as an unconventional bakery.

Interior of the old residential house studio Movedesign reimagined as an unconventional bakery

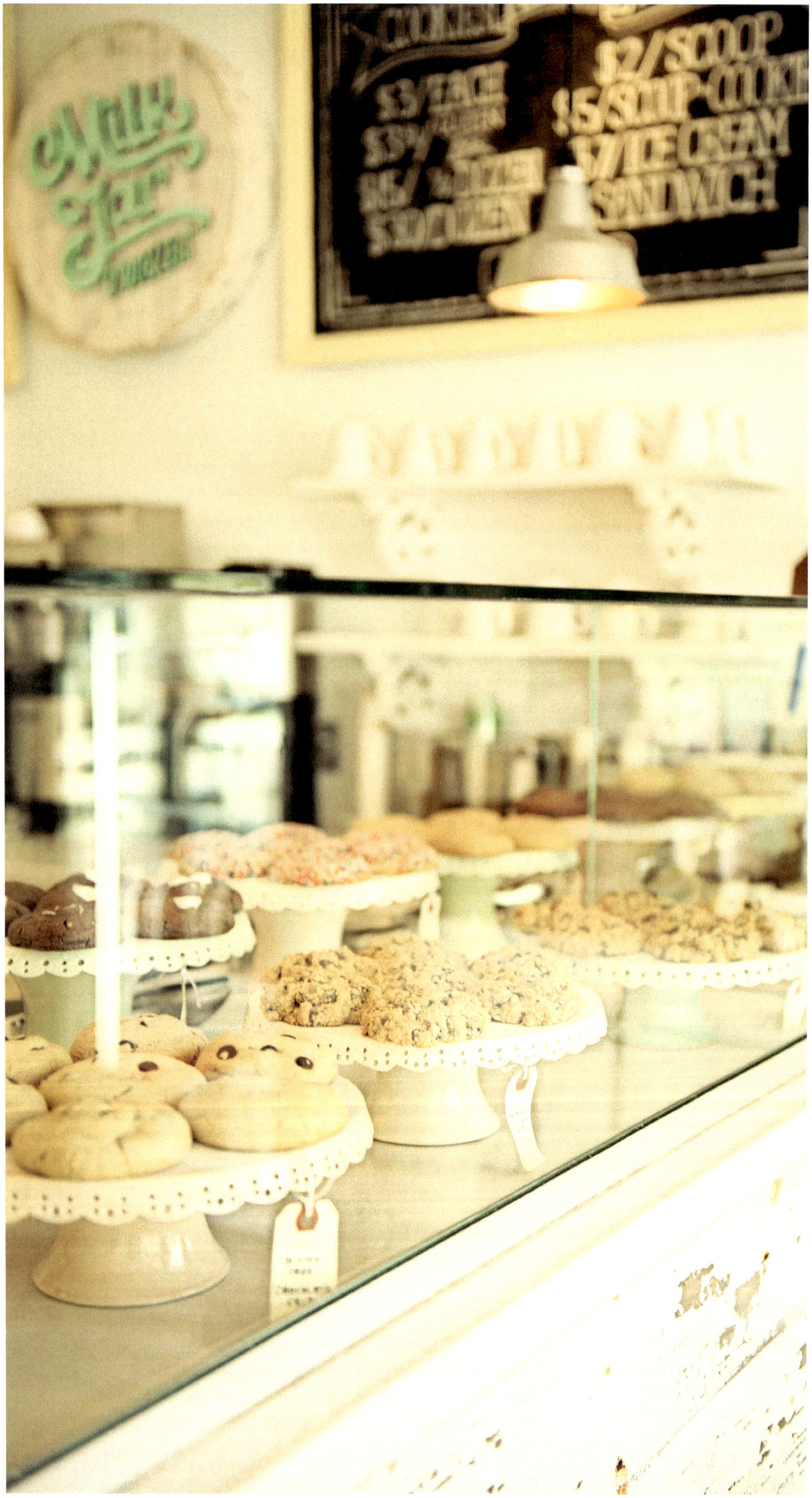

Los Angeles, CA, USA

Milk Jar Cookies

*

ABOUT: *Gourmet cookies, fresh out of the oven, baked in small batches at a quaint shop in L.A., evoking sweet memories of childhood and the best children's sweets.*

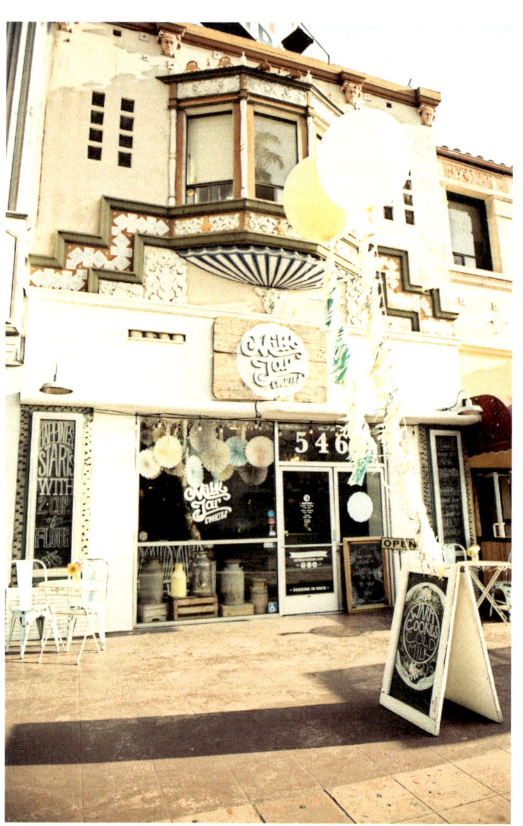

Courtney Cowan of Milk Jar Cookies and her shop's whimsical interior.

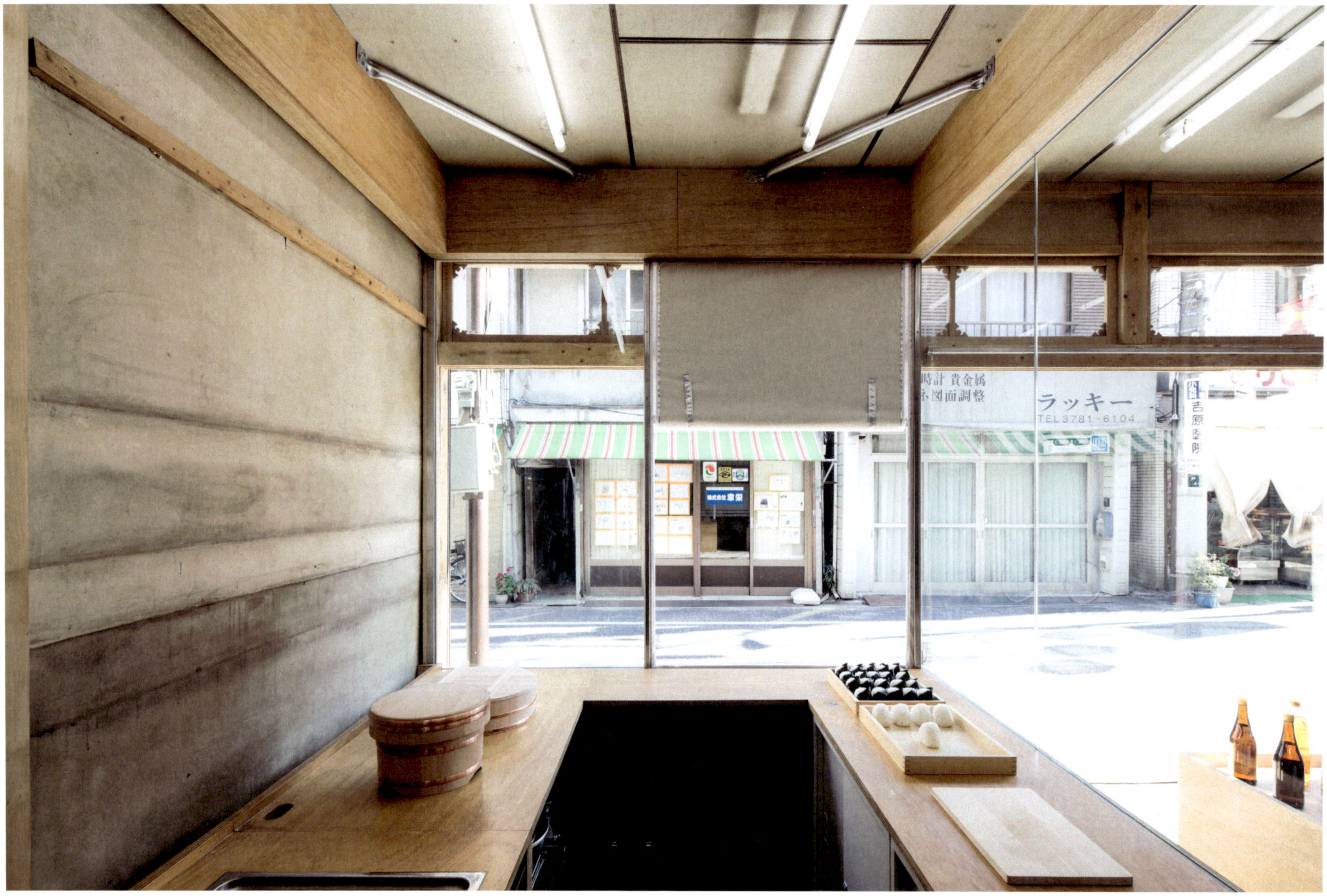
ラッキー
TEL3781-6104

8-6
お米や

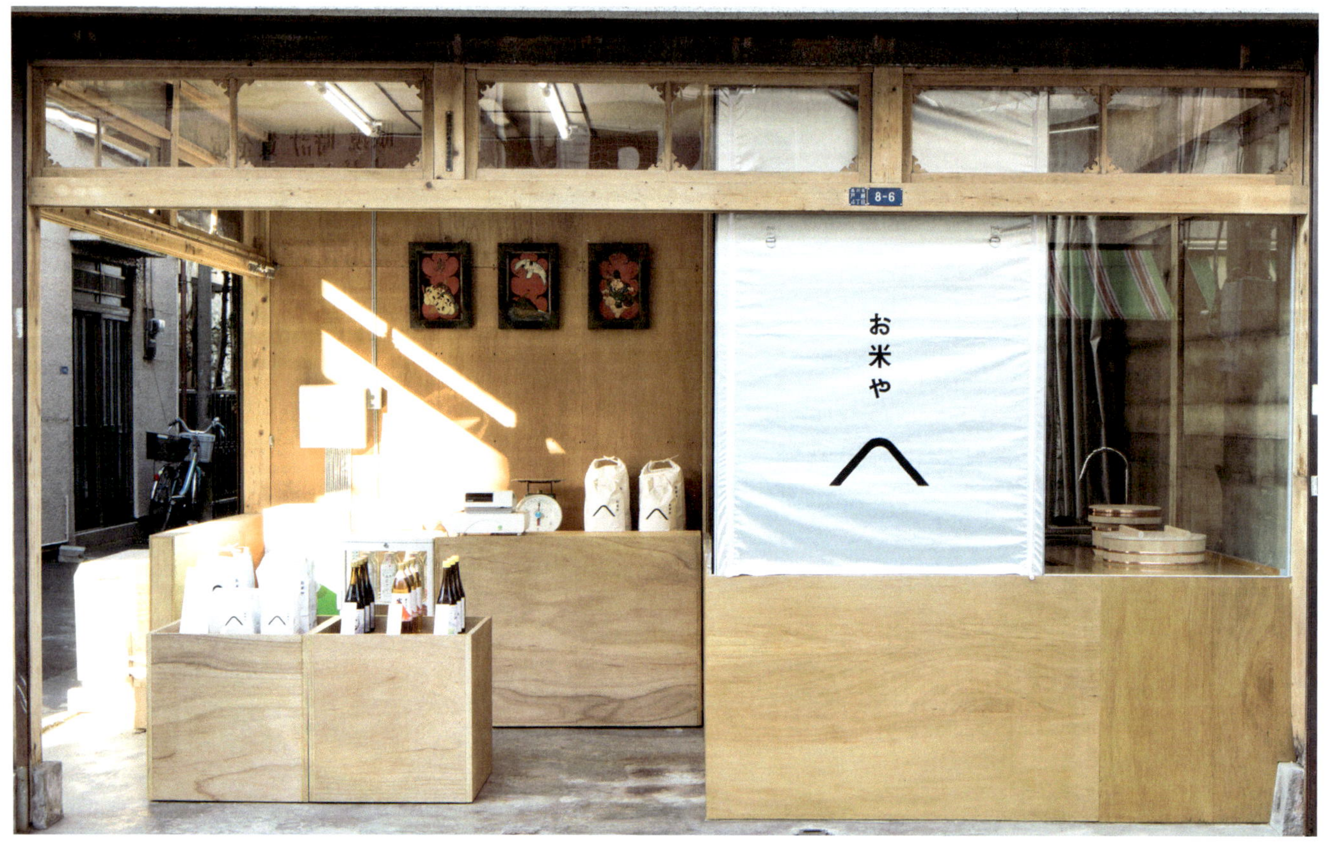

Tokyo, Japan

Okomeya

*

ABOUT: *Housed in a renovated wooden building, this modest rice shop aims to spur the revival of a street that has been in decline, sewing the fabric of the neighborhood back together.*

The Icelandic dóttir restaurant in Berlin's Mitte neighborhood espouses a design style that manages to be sleek, industrial and typically Berlin. On the ground floor of a once-abandoned office building around the corner from the renowned Unter den Linden boulevard, dóttir showcases exquisite details set against an unfinished backdrop: stripped concrete walls, high ceilings, wood-paneled floors, an open kitchen and an airy, expansive feel. Tinted and patterned cut-glass panes of different sizes symbolically separate the kitchen from the foyer. A cut-glass mirror over the bar features mounted figures and temples: somehow a cross between Ancient Greece and the Icelandic sagas.

Finally, there is Reds True Barbecue. With its neon signs, chain-link fence-enclosed open kitchen, metal shelving, and blackened, burnt timber paneling, this Leeds, U.K. restaurant is loud, brash, and fun: everything traditional BBQ is meant to be. Playing with the theme of religion, with cartoon depictions of nuns and crosses, a DJ booth that is raised like a preacher's pulpit, and restrooms with wooden doors that look a lot like confession booths, the restaurant's design firm Blacksheep sought to meld the sacred and the profane. With humor and creativity, Blacksheep's design not only matches the playful religious note of the brand (its website beckons, "Come forth believers to the original church of true barbecue"), but also poses questions about the way food and cooking can become a kind of religion, the way the food-obsessed can take on reverent, worshipful tones when they describe their last or future meal, and the fact that, when it comes down to it, all meals that include meat involve a sacrifice of sorts. ▓▓▓

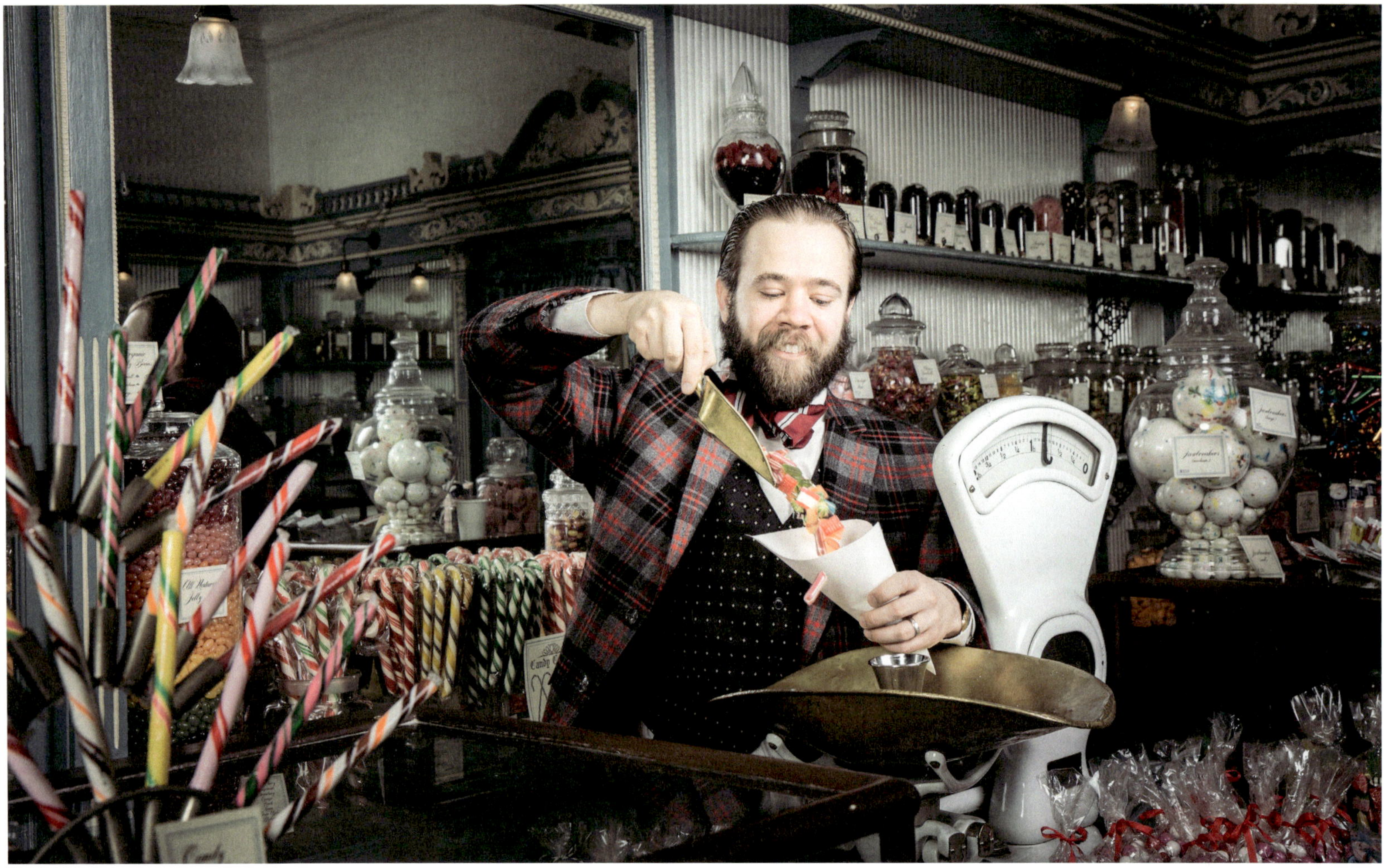

Philadelphia, USA

Shane Confectionary

*

ABOUT: *The oldest continuously operating sweet shop in America, lovingly renovated and given new personality by two children at heart: the adult owners of a nearby ice cream parlor.*

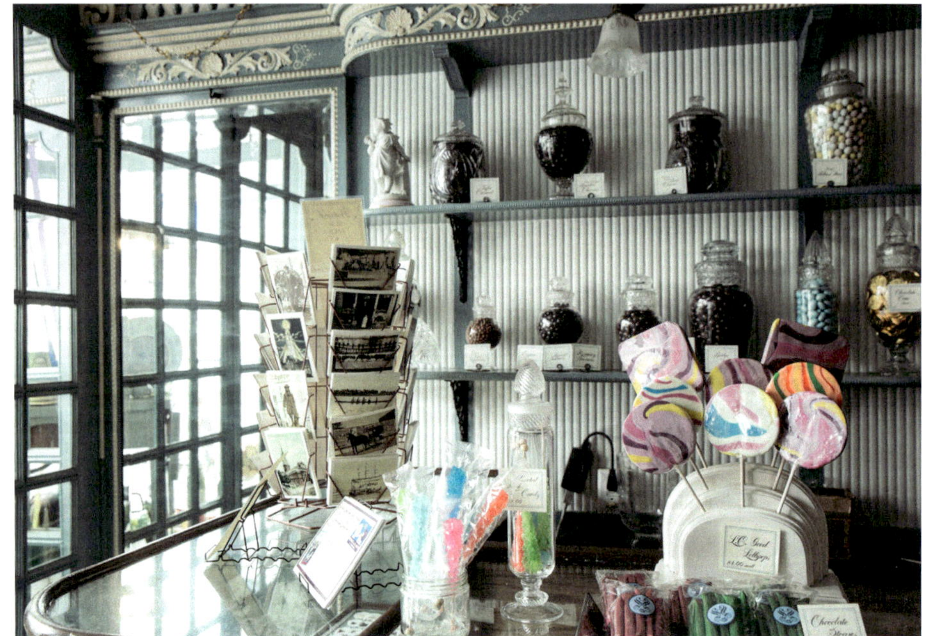

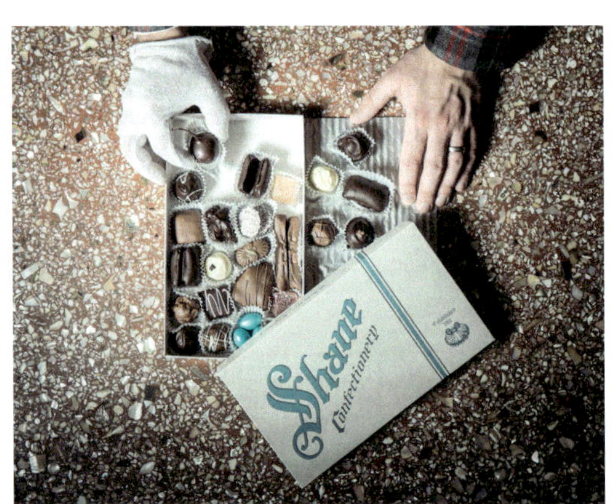

EXIT
AMOUNT
PURCHASED
NATIONAL

Shane Confectionary makes many of its own sweets in house, just like they were made 150 years ago.

Conscious Eating
Food for
in the
Thought
21st Century

It is both the blessing and the curse of the twenty-first century that we all know too much about where our food comes from. The Internet makes it easy to look up information about food producers, some of which they might rather keep secret, while well-researched tomes like Michael Pollan's *Omnivore's Dilemma* and academic-literary treatises like Jonathan Safran Foer's *Eating Animals* open our eyes to the origins of not only our meat, but all the foods we buy, grow, gather, cook or have cooked for us. The message is clear: knowledge is power, and with that power comes responsibility. The question is no longer "which came first: the chicken or the egg?" but rather, "are those chickens free-range? Are those eggs cage-free?" and above all, "are both egg and chicken happy, healthy, natural, and organic?

The amount of information available to the average consumer can be mind-boggling; it is enough to make one lose one's appetite. And yet, armed with this information, we are making better food choices for ourselves, our

families, and even our communities. Of course, there are always going to be questions of cost, and the most common argument against such conscious eating choices is that they belong squarely to the realm of the upper classes, only available to people of means. Yet this cannot be the whole story. Generations of farmers and rural communities have lived with the kinds of local and seasonal eating practices the rest of the world is rediscovering, eating only what they or their neighbors could grow. Their way of eating was neither a trend nor a choice; it had everything to do with making the most of the freshest produce when it was in season and saving up for the winter months. It wasn't about making a statement or impressing anybody; it was simply the way things were done.

Perhaps in direct response to those who say conscious eating is only for the well to do, today a new wave of entrepreneurs is harnessing the power of the Internet to connect people to each other, using foodsharing events, curated gourmet food boxes that hark back to the CSAs (community-supported agriculture) boxes of the past, educational foraging expeditions, and cooperative urban gardening to stoke interest in alternative ways of eating. Dedicated bloggers are also lending their voices to the cause, writing about their experiences with some form of specialized eating—be it vegetarian, vegan, gluten-free, paleo, flexitarian—while also projecting

Culinary Misfits' gnarled, twisted, and wholly anthropomorphous vegetables are full of character.

Berlin, Germany

Culinary Misfits

*

ABOUT: *An exploration of the intersection of design and sustainability with a primary focus on local food culture and how we can be inspired to rethink our approach to everyday food.*

Culinary Misfits takes the misshapen vegetables no one else wants and makes delicious treats out of them.

Culinary Misfits' creations are colorful, playful, and full of personality.

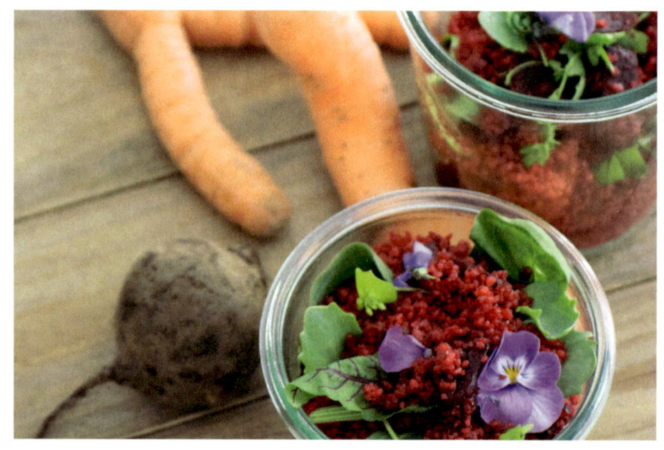

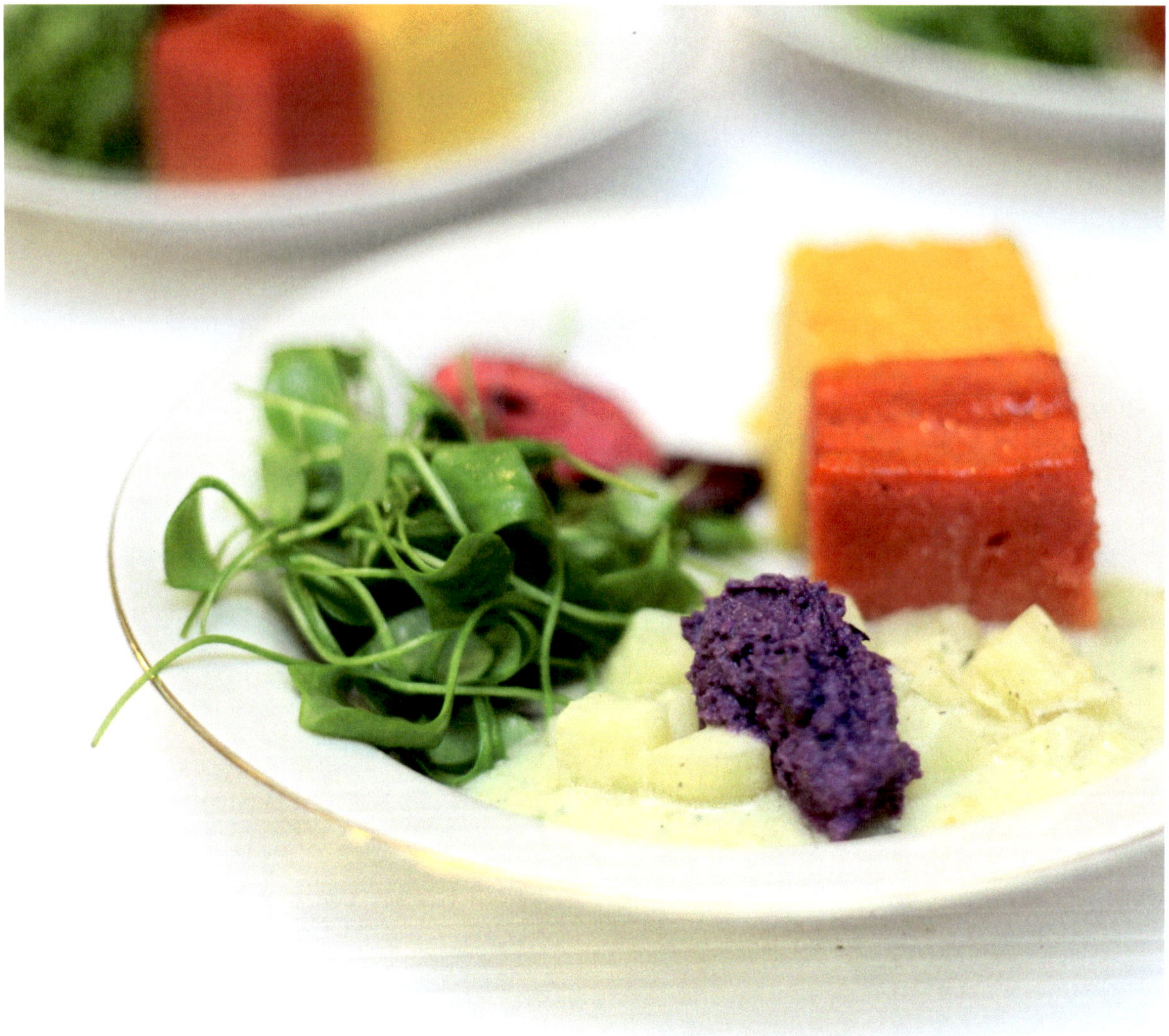

a happy, healthy, and fulfilling lifestyle at odds with the restrictive image usually associated with dieting. With the conviction that eating better is good for us as well as good for the planet, they are embracing alternative eating trends whole-heartedly, creating thousands of delicious, inventive recipes for their devoted followers.

Vegetarian and vegan restaurants, far removed from the dusty hippie cafes and health food stores of yore, are showing new customers just how exquisite, flavorful, and surprising meatless cuisine can be. One of these restaurants, the Milanese Joia, is the only Michelin-starred restaurant in Europe serving solely vegetarian, vegan, and raw cuisine. What is more, chef Pietro Leemann gives each dish flourishes of color and turns his ingredients into building blocks of abstract art, as if a child had been let loose in the kitchen and had somehow mistaken the vegetable drawer for a Lego box. Vanilla Black, a sleek, stylish vegetarian restaurant in London, is also a far cry from the hippie establishments of the past, using modern techniques and technology to give meatless dishes the exciting, contemporary treatment that is their due, with a result that is every bit as worthy of the devotion of meat eaters. London eatery Bel-Air takes

Their message: potatoes with eyes
and carrots with legs can be tasty two.

New York, NY, USA

WastED

*

ABOUT: *Blue Hill restaurant temporarily reinvented itself as wastED, a pop-up devoted to the theme of food waste and re-use.*

inspiration from the healthy eating practices of Los Angeles natives: the Shoreditch café's bright interior matches the vibrancy of its colorful salads and vegetable dishes, its goal is to make a version of fast food that can be health-conscious as well as delicious, finding "a way to brighten London's fast food scene, and bring a slice of healthy L.A. living back home."

A grassroots movement still needs its influential voices at the top of the food chain, though. One famous advocate of conscious growing, cooking, and eating practices is chef Dan Barber, of the renowned restaurants Blue Hill and Blue Hill at Stone Barns in New York. Early in 2015, Barber made a statement about waste by turning his New York restaurant into an entirely new dining concept called wastED, where food scraps that might normally have been trash were instead turned into a menu of dishes every bit as stunning as what his kitchen normally turns out. An entirely new branding concept and decorative scheme introduced the ⟩⟩

Berlin, Germany

foodXchange

*

ABOUT: *A swapping club of homemade and self-harvested food, for people who are crazy about cooking and baking and keen on bartering their edible treasures for someone else's.*

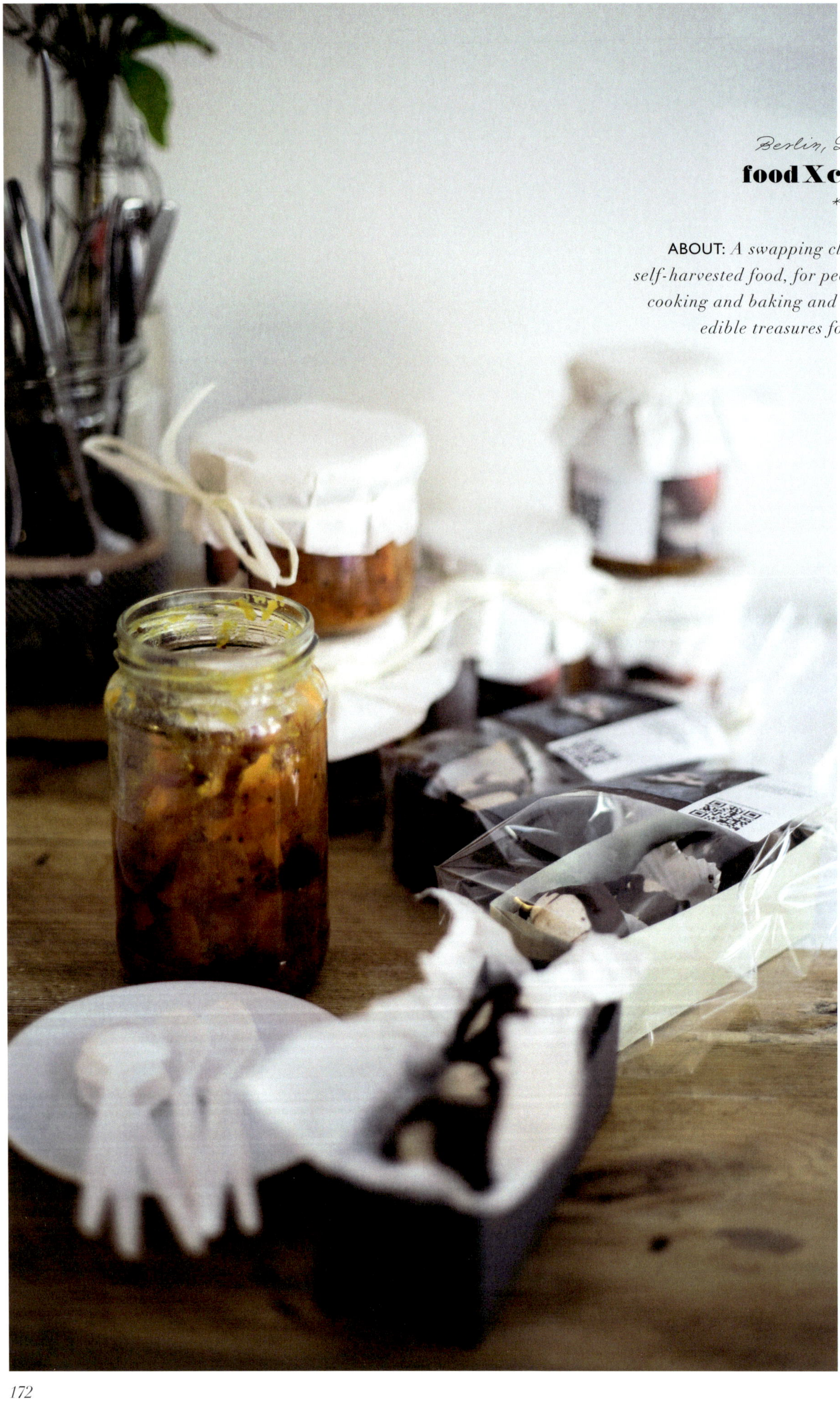

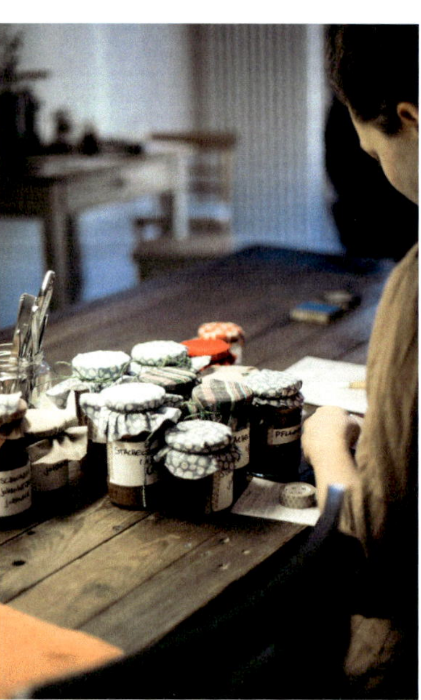

Home cooks, bakers, and picklers, unite! Berlin's foodXchange leads the way in food sharing.

FoodXchange members use the fruits of the German landscape to make products their grandmothers might have loved.

feel of a special pop-up, while small touches like candles made of beef tallow, vegetables in place of flowers on tables, and brown paper and newspaper used in place of menus and dish accouterments helped reinforce the notion of eating in a unique, entirely recycled space. The restaurant itself was quick to point out that this seemingly novel concept was in fact rooted in tradition. They were, as they said, helping "celebrate what chefs do every day on their menus (and peasant cooking has done for thousands of years): creating something delicious out of the ignored or un-coveted."

Quaint Berlin café Culinary Misfits takes a different stance, teaching us that the fight against waste can even start at the beginning of a meal instead of the end: their gnarled, twisted, and wholly anthropomorphous vegetables are full of character, and yet are all too often thrown out by supermarkets who want to project an image of agrarian perfection. Their message: potatoes with eyes and carrots with legs can be tasty too. Their medium: an eclectic décor concept that is classically Berlin: found objects

London, England
Bel-Air
*

ABOUT: *A way to brighten London's fast food scene and bring a slice of healthy L.A. living back home.*

A bit of California in London: Bel-Air's fresh, colorful and nutritious salads.

Vegetarian and vegan restaurants are far removed from the dusty hippie cafes and health food stores of yore.

and upcycled furniture enhanced by playful cartoon paintings of vegetables by local artist Matteo Dineen. "The overall effect," explains one half of the Misfits duo Tanja Krakowski, "leaves one realizing that there is much more beauty in variation than there is in having a homogenous collection of identical plates, cups, and — most of all — vegetables."

Also intent on changing the way we shop on a local level, Tokyo's FOOD & COMPANY is a self-proclaimed communal supermarket. "Sharing a delicious meal has a deeper and longer-lasting bond than one woven together with words," explain company founders Bing Bai and Maya Yatabe. "Each of us, on an almost daily basis, goes shopping and eats food. Would not the simple solution be, then, to slowly change the way in which we shop for this basic and central part of our lives?" The store is one of the first to offer organic vegetables and products in a country that is still catching on to the organic trend. Products that showcase the deep cultural roots of Japan's prefects and the great variety of what they have to offer are first and foremost; as Bai and Yatabe explain, "The 'company' in FOOD & COMPANY includes the company of our Partners (the producers of our food), our customers, and our neighbors — all

Milan, Italy

Joia

*

ABOUT: *Studying nature to represent its essence in a teasing, playful way. My cuisine is a stroll through an imaginary landscape, metaphysical, surreal, hyper-realistic, but real.*

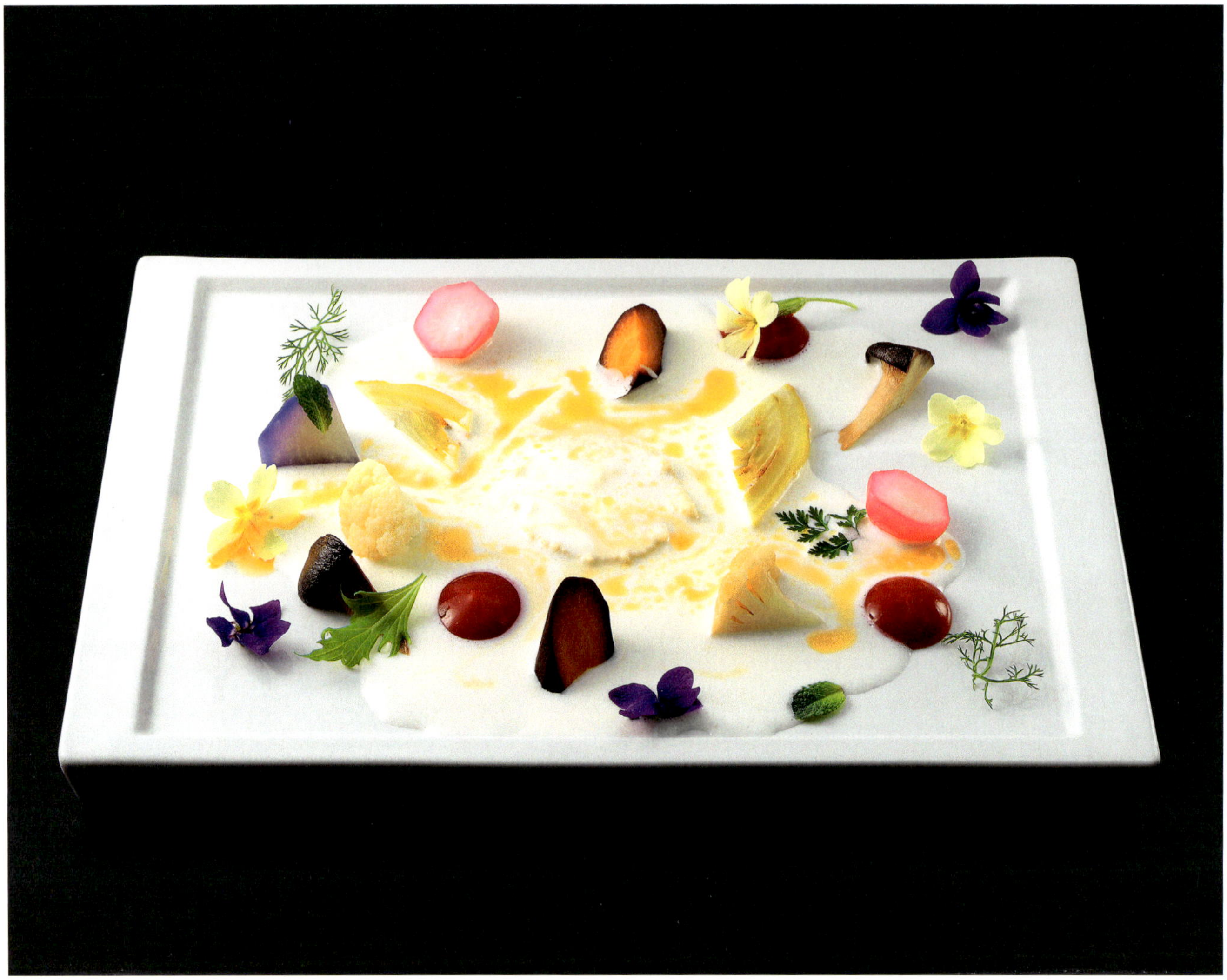

Joia is the only Michelin-starred restaurant in Europe serving solely vegetarian, vegan, and raw cuisine.

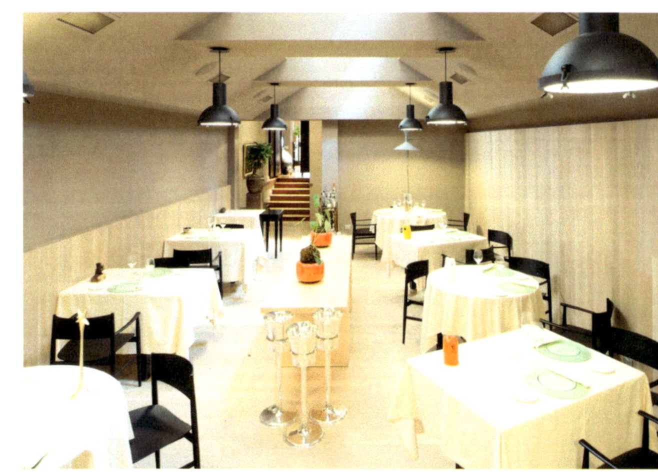

Chef Pietro Leemann of Joia in Milan celebrates the building blocks of nature in a creative and colorful way.

those to whom we are connected." In keeping with this community feel, FOOD&COMPANY aims to be far more than just a shop, the two founders will be hosting pop-up dinners, workshops, and panel discussions in an effort to bring the neighborhood in — one more way the supermarket of the future will be far more than just a place to stock up on groceries.

Food exchanges are another way to encourage an appreciation for community while championing homemade foods and the conservation of leftovers. Their social aspect makes them feel a bit like the sewing groups and quilting circles of yore. FoodXchange Berlin was born out of a desire to bring people together who make things with their hands, leading to an exchange of know-how and enthusiasm, and ultimately leaving participants with something beautiful to take home. Although foodXchange chapters exist all over the world, it was almost inevitable that the Berlin version, headed by Berlin food consultants Cathrin Brandes and Pamela Dorsch,, would reflect a particularly seasonal ethos, with participants using the fruits of the German landscape to make products their grandmothers might have loved.

Elderflower liqueur, apple cake, gooseberry jam, dried mushrooms, pickled garlic, all manor of nuts and roots from the garden: these are just a few of the things that have appeared at Brandes's frequent gatherings, which see a mixture of recognizable faces and hopeful newcomers, all with the goal of trading their own delicious products and learning how others made theirs. Participants are allowed the first half of the event to talk amongst themselves, ask questions about product sourcing and methods of creation, and begin to barter. Then, the trading begins. The result is a feeling of liberation akin to what pioneers must have felt

The simple, rustic interior of Vanilla Black belies its inventive vegetarian cuisine.

London, England
Vanilla Black
*
ABOUT: "We are passionate about redefining contemporary non-meat cuisine by experimenting with original flavour combinations and modern techniques."

upon surviving their first year in the wilderness; you have grown or made something with your own two hands and it's good enough to trade for something else. You have by-passed the global marketplace and refuted the workings of Capitalism to indulge in something that feels truly revolutionary and yet somehow, comfortingly old-fashioned.

Food exchanges all over the world have something of this spirit about them; of course, they do not all operate the way foodXchange Berlin does, but they are all aimed at making sure food gets into the hands of people who will use and appreciate it, whether it be rounding

New York, NY, USA

Quinciple

*

ABOUT: *Working directly with more than 100 farmers, Quinciple delivers curated boxes all over New York. Each box contains hand-picked ingredients that reflect the best of what's in season.*

The local and seasonal products in Quinciple boxes are the result of close relationships with farmers built up over years.

Food & Company

*

ABOUT: *FOOD & COMPANY is a grocery store created through the meeting of like-minded friends with the common goal of changing the world through everyday experiences and rituals.*

up restaurant leftovers to feed to hungry families, creating an app that will connect home cooks with an excess of goods to those who may not have enough, or even getting food enthusiasts to share recipes and tips that will help others replicate what they've cooked. The spirit of generosity is there, it's up to us to know what to do with it.

"Sharing a delicious meal has a deeper and longer-lasting bond than one woven together with words."

Food &
company
FOOD GUIDELINE:
F.L.O.S.S.
fresh, local,
ORGANIC,
seasonal,
sustainable.

Rediscovering
Back to
Breakfast and
Childhood
Other Things we once Loved

No doubt about it: what we choose to eat has a lot to do with what we ate in our childhoods. We celebrate a milestone birthday, and find ourselves remembering that sickeningly sweet but oh-so-delicious cake we had at our number ten; we come down with a cold and long for mom's chicken noodle soup. Perhaps, unlike any meal we grab for lunch or eat at a restaurant in the evening, what we eat at home is particularly molded by this form of culinary nostalgia: when we are away from the public eye and not susceptible to the whims of friends, colleagues or even dates — when we are simply alone or with select loved ones, within the four comforting walls of our own homes, that's when we choose what we know, what we remember, what simply makes us feel good. So it is not surprising that breakfast can be the most comforting meal of all. When done wrong, it can be nothing more than a cup of coffee as we run out the door. When done right, however, it is a quiet, meditative, and deeply pleasurable way to spend your first waking

What Should I Eat For Breakfast Today?

*

ABOUT: *A blog about cooking, baking, exploring, and enjoying the slow moments in life, including a quiet, contemplative breakfast of homemade treats before the day begins.*

hour: just out of bed, still in the most comfortable clothes you'll wear all day, breakfast is a time to come out of your dreams and into reality, taking stock of the day ahead, preferably with the help of something delicious.

Take it from blogger Marta Greber, who, with a blog title that is a simple question, gets at the heart of what delights us about breakfast. Your parents called it the most important meal of the day, and when you were a student, you probably thought you could skip it altogether. But in recent years, getting up early enough to enjoy a fulfilling first meal has increasingly been seen as an indication of one's values. Marta's blog, *What Should I Eat For Breakfast Today?* embraces those early morning hours wholeheartedly, making it look like a joy, not a drag, to wake up for breakfast.

With her combination of recipes, cafe reviews, and life musings accompanied by colorful and whimsical photography that is nevertheless somewhat grainy and analogue, Marta celebrates a time of day that many see but few stop to enjoy. Her carefully curated guides to cities like Barcelona and Lisbon make it even easier to understand her aesthetic: here is a woman who goes through life with slow wonder, very often accompanied by her partner Tomasz and baby daughter Mia, taking every moment to savor a spontaneous, home-baked cinnamon raisin twist, an early morning breakfast in the park with a carrot, banana, and orange cake pulled out of the oven just an hour ago, or a lesson in the art of making Pasteis de Nata, Portugal's favorite pastry.

Her stories, while heartfelt and personal, always include a recipe, so even when her milestone moments might not exactly match up with yours, you can still follow her instructions to bake beetroot crepes, ricotta cakes, or an exquisite almond tart with strawberry-lemon compote. Marta's conviction that you should make every single moment in life delicious—and savor it the right way—harks back to an earlier time. Her website is a guidebook to discovering that sense of childhood wonder in everyday moments all over again.

Meanwhile, the Tokyo-based café World Breakfast All Day takes another look at the first meal of the day, from a global

The first meal of the day is once again the most important one on the blog,
What Should I Eat For Breakfast Today?

Hot Milk Lab

*

ABOUT: *A micro laboratory for heating, mixing and experimenting by heating milk and adding aromas, spices and other ingredients to extend and develop the drinking experience.*

point of view. With the conviction that what people eat for breakfast can reveal much more than just their personal histories — it can also tell you quite a lot about their culture, nationality, traditions, and beliefs — the café's approach is almost anthropological in its desire to nourish both the body and the intellect. Their charming concept is so simple, it leads one to question why it has not been done before: every two months on a rotating basis, the café offers several dishes that represent the breakfast of a certain country. Visit any time, from early morning to late dinner, and be prepared to be served waffles from Belgium, hummus, falafel, babaganoush and pita from Jordan, a Pão Francês sandwich and papaya salad from Brazil, *idli* rice patties, curry, and chutneys from India, or traditional eggs, beans, and toast from England.

The crew of World Breakfast All Day see it as their mission to fight the globalization of breakfast, which becomes more and more standardized as multi-national corporations

Tokyo, Japan

Ganori

*

ABOUT: *"Granola offers excellent nutritional balance to prepare for the day ahead, and it's a charming breakfast. I saw an opportunity in trying to develop a taste for this in Japan."*

spread the tainted gospel of sugary cereals and high-calorie energy bars free of real nutrients. As they put it, "The national breakfasts of the world are rich in history, yet many are now fading away as people opt to start their day with generic meals." Their tiny, eclectic café space is full of color, thanks to a range of products from around the world that grace its shelves, and the feeling is one of laid-back indulgence paired with a pinch of childhood silliness. After all, having breakfast at dinnertime was the dream back when our parents were telling us what to do.

Just as this Tokyo café brings international breakfast traditions to Japan, a very western breakfast style is also coming to town: granola. That crunchy, rich, sweet and savory cornucopia that can be adapted to fit any diet, palate, or whim, is inspiring Japanese cooks and foodies who aim to make the

cereal their very own, yielding some interesting new combinations. The Tokyo shop Ganori is one of its purveyors, presenting their granola mixes in beautiful packaging, while their store displays make it easy to see granola as a malleable breakfast, able to be bent to one's wishes, mixed and matched, played with, and invented anew. Japanese ingredients include black soybeans, burdock root, and black sesame seeds. Different types of milk (regular, soy, strawberry) are available to add new flavor to your granola mix, and fresh fruit toppings are par for the course. Just a few years ago, shops like Ganori and World Breakfast All Day would have been unthinkable — breakfast establishments in many parts of the world were envisioned as either greasy spoons (long-running, busy, no-frills coffee shops), diners, or tiny street stands — places to eat quickly when you did not have enough time or energy to prepare a meal at home. Now, breakfast is getting its due as an artisanal meal every bit as crucial as the rest.

Taking another, slightly different stab at a breakfast staple is Sebastian Bergne, with his compact, self-contained Hot Milk Lab. Outlining his idea for this project, Bergne

Ganori's homemade granolas have given Japan a taste
for the classic baked breakfast item.

World Breakfast All Day

*

ABOUT: *"We offer you the chance to indulge in traditional morning meals that are filled with delicious and intriguing subtleties, sweeping you up and away on an international voyage."*

Typical breakfast in Tahiti

Typical breakfast in Russia

explains, "The nutritional content of milk has guaranteed its value as an everyday drink for centuries. Its water, protein, and fat content make it ideal as a vehicle for mixing with a variety of flavorings. When gently heated, its ability to absorb aromas and combine with other ingredients is increased still further."

Balanced on two smooth, wooden trays built specifically for them, a selection of measuring, mixing, and tasting vessels are lined up and exhibited, like a magician presenting his tricks. A second tray displays a line of slim beakers holding the various raw ingredients for flavorings: cinnamon, anis, flaxseed, chocolate, and in a grown-up twist, even bird's eye chili.

Holiday leftovers for breakfast in the USA
Next Page: Typical breakfast in Croatia

A dish of frilly French *sablé* (short-bread cook-ies) sits alongside, as if underlining the notion that, although this is designed like a highly pre-cise scientific experiment, it is really envisioned as a portal back to childhood — a kit for adults who want to have fun with a drink that is as fundamental as, well, mother's milk.

Meanwhile, Melbourne's Mörk Chocolate takes a drink that is as fundamental to child-hood happiness as milk and turns it into a gourmet product that flatters the adult palate. Australia has long been home to some of the most advanced specialty coffee-roasters in the southern hemisphere, and Mörk saw an opening for another hot drink that deserved its due: hot chocolate. As founders Josefin Zernell and Kiril Shaginov explain, "Mörk Chocolate started as an idea of creating a specialty dark drinking choc-olate culture in Melbourne to meet and inspire the growing specialty coffee and cafe culture."

Their chocolate is sweetened only with co-conut blossom sugar, and sold in four varieties: Junior Dark 50%, Original Dark 70%, Even Darker 85% and Dark Milk & River Salt 65%. Solid chocolate has been revered as a delicacy, a costly gift and an aphrodisiac worldwide for centuries, their concept hints, but now it's time to give the liquid version — in many ways its polar opposite: warming, comforting and child-like — its proper due.

On the other hand, the craft beer cul-ture is also going strong down under, and

World Breakfast All Day serves breakfast from all over the world, including this typical Peruvian breakfast

Breakfast in Bulgaria

Breakfast in Belgium

Breakfast in Mexico

Breakfast in Vietnam

Breakfast in Finland

Mörk Chocolate

*

ABOUT: *Mörk Chocolate started [with]
an idea of creating a specialty dark drinking
chocolate culture in Melbourne to meet
and inspire the growing specialty coffee
and cafe culture.*

the Mörk Chocolate Brew House (the company's concept store) is a worthy homage to craft beer that also pokes a bit of fun at its own seriousness. The bright white interior is adorned with wooden shelves featuring the chocolate mixtures and other housemade treats, its smooth walls marked only by a variety of spigots that dispense not hops and barley, but rather hot and chilled chocolate beverages. Meanwhile, a clean counter space mimicking a bartop is used to showcase different brewing methods and prepare customers their drinks, which you can be sure, will take them back to that moment in childhood when they'd just gotten off a sled after a first snowfall and stripped their sodden winter layers off, to be met with a steaming, fragrant, soothing cup of hot chocolate.

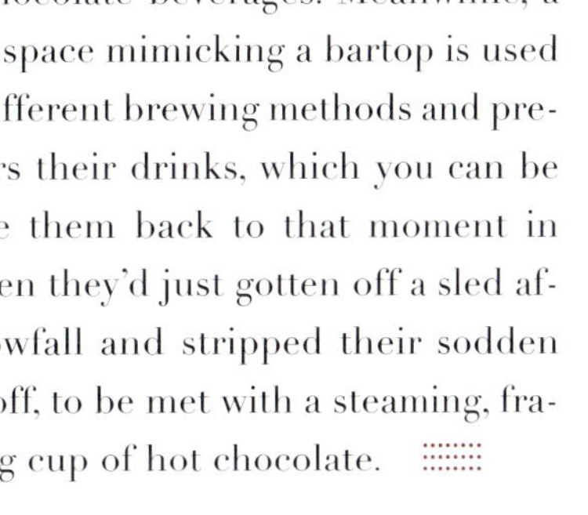

Artisanal hot chocolate from bean to cup, by Mörk Chocolate

The Courage to Forage

Seeking Out for Edible Delights in Fields, Forests, and Seas

These days, chefs and food lovers are always on the lookout for local, organic, and self-grown food, and many of them have a secret: foraging. Although the quantity and quality of found edible plants can vary widely by city, more and more urban dwellers are creating entire meals based on what they gather just beyond city limits — or what can be found between the cracks and folds of the urban fabric itself.

Perhaps it's about regaining the thrill of discovery we experienced as children — the first time we realized where an egg comes from, or saw a tree go from blossom to fruit in a few short months and realized how apples were made. Or perhaps it goes even further back, to an instinct left over from eons ago, when we did not know how to grow our own food yet, and instead had to find it in the forest. Nevertheless, spurred on by both healthy eating bloggers and chefs — notably René Redzepi of Copenhagen restaurant Noma, and Magnus Nilsson of Fäviken in Sweden — more foragers are on the lookout for the rarest edible plants, stalks, ≫≫≫

A rainbow of flavors and colors direct from the sea, via the Cornish Seaweed Company

roots, and flowers, and making something delicious with them.

When Kristen Rasmussen — a founder of the California collective Berkeley Open Source Food along with Philip B. Stark and Tom Carlso — named her blog Rooted Food, the double meaning was no doubt intentional: foods that come from the ground are also closely connected to our own roots. The oft-parroted warning not to eat anything with an ingredient your grandma would not recognize has its roots in a similar presumption: the best food for us should come out of the ground around us, and should require minimal effort to taste delicious.

A branch of this trend extends into high-tech territory as well. The obsession with getting back to our roots and looking to the ground for sustenance is paired with an element of social and environmental consciousness. What if, at some point not too far in the future, the foods we rely on are no longer available? The solution: go back to your roots — back to the forest — and look to the ground. Conversely, an interest in new gadgets and new ways of preparing foods to preserve their highest percentage of nutrition — reaching

Cornwall, England

The Cornish Seaweed Company

*

ABOUT: *"We are a small team of passionate seaweeders who sustainably hand harvest and traditionally sun dry a fine selection of Cornish seaweeds from our rugged coastline."*

its apex in the Vitamix blender, which has achieved cult status — means many plants are being subjected to ever-newer technologies to maximize their properties. After all, what easier, better, more straightforward way to consume foraged grasses, plants and herbs than sticking them all in a blender and drinking them? Hence the advent of the so-called green smoothie: made from all those living things we gather in the wild, transformed into something pretty far from their roots.

Modern foraging should lie somewhere in between, taking the best elements of both past and present to design a new best practice: tracking the seasons and weather conditions (with an app, perhaps), spotting signs that the timing is best for blueberries, for instance, or certain types of mushrooms, and then going out into the world with a sack, a knife, or a pair of scissors to harvest. Then comes the most creative part: cooking, baking, pickling and preserving what has been found. This is where the most up-to-date methods of food preparation can be used; this is where ancient foraging techniques and long-studied plant knowledge can influence the newest trends in eating.

Take, for example, the simple syrup on Rasmussen's blog, made from buds of wild chamomile, also known as pineapple weed for its sweet, almost tropical scent. In late spring in temperate climates, this weed grows profligately next to dusty country roads and through cracks in the concrete. Its stalks reach just to the ankle but no further, its yellow flowers not quite bright enough to be noticed unless you are looking for them. Yet their buds contain an essential oil concentrated enough to release a quite intense, fruity and planty flavor into boiling sugar water, making for syrup that is equal parts striking and soothing. The resulting wild chamomile syrup makes for a perfect old-fashioned and somewhat medicinal cocktail when paired with gin, following the current bartending craze for old-school syrups and bitters.

Another monument to early spring, the wildly popular ramps — also called wild garlic or bear's garlic — are entirely edible, from stem to leaf to flower, and can be used in an endless variety of dishes. It's showed up in everything from pizzas and pastas to omelets, but the best way to preserve its flavor long-term is to chop it up in a blender with olive oil, parmesan cheese, and pine nuts or walnuts, making a pesto that can go directly onto pasta, be spread on top of bread, or diluted with oil for a green salad vinaigrette with a particularly sharp bite.

And nothing can top the surprising, slightly danger-inflected pleasure of eating stinging nettles — picked carefully with gloves, and boiled to tame them. Nettles are a great source of vitamin C, iron, potassium, calcium, and (unusually for a plant) protein. What is more, nettles can be consumed in countless ways — cooked as one would cook spinach, blended into a smoothie, or dried and made into a soothing herbal tea. A quiche with nettles would not be out of the question, and a pureed soup of nettles would benefit from the addition of crème fraiche, quark, or goat cheese and some toasted seeds or spices.

As if there weren't enough treasures to be found on land, a new generation of food lovers — spearheaded by some pretty forward-thinking companies — are discovering the nutritional and culinary benefits of seaweed. The mysterious, slimy vegetable can sometimes seem to be half saltwater, half alien creature. Slick, tempting, foreboding meadows of it wavered just under the surface of the ocean's murkiest shoals, feeding our childhood fantasies. Now adults, we have realized it can feed us in a more literal way.

In a treatise on its website, the Cornish Seaweed Company waxes lyrical on the nutritional and medicinal benefits of seaweed, explaining their preternaturally high levels of vitamins and minerals as a result of pure survival of the fittest: "Seaweeds live in ▷▷▷

Skeins of seaweed can be cooked like spaghetti, seaweed slivers can be added to salads, and dried seaweed acts as an umami seasoning.

Berkeley Open Source Food

*

ABOUT: *Foraging experts who work with the communities, chefs, restaurants, and farms in and around Berkeley to promote safe and sustainable foraging practices.*

a very complex environment and are exposed to extreme and rapidly changing environmental conditions. To survive and adapt to these conditions, they have developed special mechanisms that are unique or are present at much higher concentrations than in any other plant or animal."

For those looking to make something out of these natural wonders, beyond the conventional Japanese staples of miso soup and sushi rolls, the company presents a variety of recipes that are meant not to encompass everything seaweed has to offer, but rather to serve as inspiration for those looking to incorporate it into their diets. Unsurprisingly, skeins of seaweed can be cooked like spaghetti, seaweed slivers can be added to salads, pastas, fritters and potatoes, and dried seaweed acts as an umami seasoning, whether alone, mixed in with butter, or added to flaky sea salt.

But is it really wise to encourage foraging in ever-larger enthusiastic groups of eaters? Will it not lead to a state of affairs that is purely unsustainable? In fact, most plants that are foraged from the wild have been growing contentedly for years without human interference. They are much heartier than most garden- or farm-grown crops as they very often must survive and thrive in a fully heterogeneous biosphere, competing with other plants on the forest floor and developing elaborate mechanisms to keep from getting eaten by animals. Still, it's best to be cautious when it comes to found edibles.

Then comes the most creative part: cooking, baking, pickling and preserving what has been found.

A few mindful steps will help keep the legions of fiddleheads, morels, and berries flourishing:

1 Use the correct tools. Wild plants, though strong in bunches, can also be quite fragile when taken stalk by stalk. In order to guarantee the plant is not harmed and can regenerate itself, a clean and precise cut is almost always necessary. Know when you need scissors, when you need a sharp knife, and when you might want gloves, twine, or other props for your foraging adventures.

2 Tell few people about your foraging spots—and only the right people. It may seem unfair at best, downright greedy at worst, but by making sure your entire town is not hot on your heels, you will guarantee that colonies of edible goods can replenish themselves. Tell one or two enthusiastic friends, take them along if you must, but do not draw a map with X marking the spot, or pretty soon the X will not mark anything anymore.

3 Take just enough, and leave the roots whenever possible. There are those who prize the mild white bulbs of wild garlic far more than their stalks and leaves, but take too many of those bulbs and there will be nothing left next year. Remove all the elderflower clusters from the tree, and there will be none left to grow into elderberries in the fall (a delicacy in their own right).

What with all the high-end molecular gastronomy and low-end processed foods, it is only natural that we should want to return to our roots. Venturing out into the wild and seeing what we find there is just one way to do that, but it is perhaps the most egalitarian: free, easy, and open to all who have courage, an adventurous spirit, and a spark of curiosity.

New Meat

The Carnivores

Take a Stand

It's been a tough few years for meat-eaters. Well, call it a tough few decades. First came the news that red meat is bad for you. Then came the vegetarian onslaught: actually, all meat is bad for you. The guilt tripping, the silent treatment, the disdain were all next. If you still eat meat these days, you are supposed to pretend you do so begrudgingly, sparingly, and above all, rarely. You are supposed to feel ashamed.

It was only a matter of time before the meat-eaters fought back. And what soldiers they are: armed with axes, cleavers, hooks, and specialty knives, this aproned, often bearded group of specialists unashamedly broadcasts their loyalties, posing with pigs' heads, cows' feet, and all manner of innards the greater majority of us would rather just not think about. In the end, the sentiment that fuels this "bones out" theatricality is a desire for authenticity: for far too long, they argue, meat was a bloodless, sanitized thing: a slab of red covered in plastic, to be placed without a thought on the supermarket cart. Being a conscious eater these

The Rough Kitchen

*

ABOUT: *"An initiative by two carnivores with heart and soul, we grill, smoke and roast our products in an attempt to communicate a simple message: Eat meat. Be happy."*

days does not entail foregoing meat entirely, but it does entail knowing where your meat comes from, caring about how an animal is raised, prepped and butchered, and, once and for all, facing the fact that the act of eating is often inextricably linked with the act of killing.

Meat preparation used to be a secretive process, but today meat-makers are coming into the light to show pride in their products and keep their customers well-informed and satisfied.

The nose-to-tail movement we see today was born out of the same conviction that has us eating seasonally and locally: in the past, when our ancestors were lucky enough to have an animal to eat — either by hunting them in the wild or raising domesticated ones — they did not want to let any of it go to waste. Children learn this early on when they learn about the customs of many ancient cultures: meat was cured and smoked, bones were made into jewelry and toys for children, animal hides became clothing and were stretched over supports to make homes. It is perhaps the romanticized notion of being pioneers or settlers in uncharted

Like many new meat purveyors, The Rough Kitchen's products come from sustainably, humanely raised animals.

regions—combined with the conviction that wastefulness is next to sinfulness—that is at the heart of the nose-to-tail movement.

It's a movement that includes farmers, butchers, smokers, grillers and an assortment of master chefs all working together. As with many other movements, its goal is to educate as much as it is to feed hungry customers. The Rough Kitchen, for example, employs a motto that is as self-assured as it is reassuring, especially to carnivores who may still feel those pangs of guilt: "Eat meat, be happy" could be seen as a clarion call to those who refuse to swear off animal products, and the Amsterdam company has made it their mission to promote this middle line, focusing on quality breeds like Berkshire Pigs that

Amsterdam's The Rough Kitchen reacquaints the Dutch population with local, humanely raised, delicious meat.

BORRELBITES
TASTING PLATTERS

were raised humanely, locally, and sustainably. In another part of the Dutch capital, sausage-makers Brandt & Levie offer a succession of dried and fresh sausages based on the appreciation, enthusiasm, and know-how they have accumulated from travels to charcuterie-heavy countries like Germany, Italy, and even Morocco. Like many in this new crop of meat-makers, their goal is not just to sell their handcrafted products, but rather to educate the public on how sausage is made, the proper way to cook it, and the best storage methods.

The meat deli Lennart & Bror in Stockholm is revitalizing an old concept: decades ago, before factory farming and industrialized meat production, small, personal shops weren't part of a new trend; they were just the norm. And butchers were at the top of the social

Stockholm, Sweden

Lennart & Bror

*

ABOUT: *A reimagining of an old-fashioned, neighborhood delicatessen, offering quality meats, grocery staples, and a friendly, local vibe.*

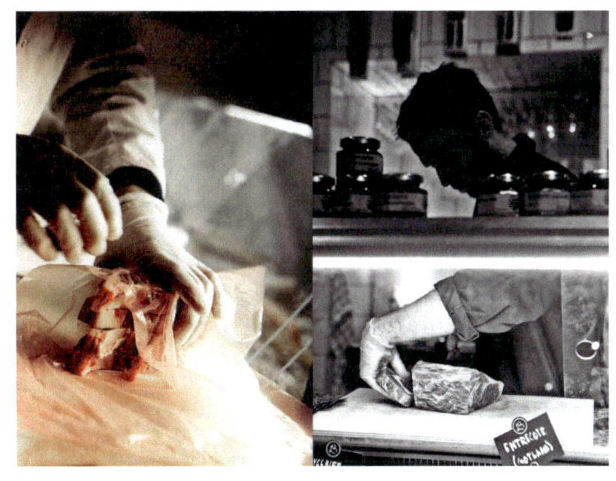

Hood Food creates themed dinners from local and organic products, including pork from local pigs.

Hood Food

*

ABOUT: *Hood Food is devoted to using offbeat but simple products to make locally sourced meals that are as delicious as they are inspiring. Hood, of course, is short for neighborhood.*

heap, providing a crucial and valuable product to their customers in shops that often served as focal points for neighborhood life. Lennart & Bror reimagines this localized concept with a clean, tiled space that offers customers an array of meats cut to order, as well as homemade sausages served in a crusty roll with sauerkraut, to eat in store.

Across the pond, The Meat Hook has set up shop in Brooklyn. More of a meat collective than a simple shop, its multiple proprietors all have their specialties, passions and backgrounds, and work together to bring New Yorkers beef, lamb, and pork products, as well as an extensive list of what they call Classy Sausages like German bratwurst or sweet Italian sausage, and

Trashy Sausages—new creations like Bahn Mi, an ode to the classic Vietnamese sandwich, or the Cougar: pork and bacon spiked with scallions, soy sauce, brown sugar, and red pepper flakes. They project a playful vibe, but their website makes it clear how serious they are: "From farm visits to pick our animals for the next month's slaughter to chatting up regulars

A series of dishes showcase and celebrate the pig in all its glory.

The Meat Hook

*

ABOUT: *Uniting a collection of passionate food entrepreneurs who work to maintain close connections with farmers and provide customers with the highest quality meat.*

The Meat Hook is a meat collective that aims to built lasting relationships with both farmers and customers.

at the counter, everything we do is for the purpose of properly representing our farmer's hard work, deep knowledge and quality animals. We never forget that without them we are just another bunch of jerks selling pork chops."

Hood Food is a pop-up dining experience in Zürich concentrating exclusively on locally sourced ingredients (hence the "Hood," as in "neighborhood"). For their *Homage an Das Schwein* (Homage to the Pig) dinner, they sourced their pigs directly from the farmyard and created a series of dishes showcasing pork in all its glory, from the classic head cheese and sliced ham to a formidable plate of *choucroute*. The result was a multi-faceted celebration of an amazing animal that has been nourishing generations of humans across many cultures.

Bringing meat consumption into the home is Carnivore Club, which takes the idea of an artisanal food box and transforms

For Dutch company Brandt & Levie, sausage-making is an art.

Brandt & Levie

*

ABOUT: *Dutch artisinal sausage makers who have traveled the world to sample the best varieties and reinvent them for Amsterdam.*

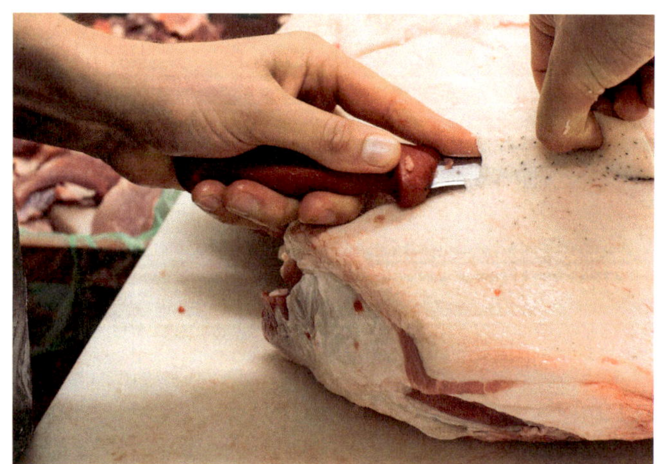

it into something solely for the discerning carnivore. Members receive a monthly or bimonthly box showcasing the cured meats of a single producer. One month it could be Spanish Chorizo, the next South African cured meats, then artisanal jerky from New York, or samples from a Miami smokehouse. In the process, Carnivore Club supports ethical animal husbandry and slaughtering practices, and aims to excite customers about the incredible variety of cured meats that exist in the world — something that, with our chilled supermarket cases and processed meat products, we can all too easily forget.

Carnivore Club

*

ABOUT: *Curated, monthly cured meat boxes for the discerning carnivore, sourcing small, artisanal producers to deliver Russian, Italian, Canadian, and French varieties.*

Charcuterie in a box: a glimpse of the offerings from monthly meat subscription service the Carnivore Club.

The Delicious

A Companion to New Food Culture

This book was conceived, edited, and designed by Gestalten.

Edited by Giulia Pines, Robert Klanten, and Sven Ehmann
Preface and texts by Giulia Pines

Creative direction by Robert Klanten and Sven Ehmann
Cover and layout by Sarah Peth
Editorial management by Silvena Ivanova
Text edited by Noelia Hobeika
Proofreading by Transparent Language Solutions

Cover photography by Marta Greber
Back cover photography: Marta Greber (top left);
clockwise from middle left: Julia Gartland,
Héctor Hernández, Haim Yosef, Saskia van Osnabrugge,
Chefs Club by Food & Wine, Héctor Hernández

Typefaces: Didot by Pierre Didot/François Rappo,
Fette Bauersche Antiqua by Peter Wiegel,
Gill Sans by Eric Gill, Emily In White III
by Julia Sysmäläinen

Printed by Offsetdruckerei Grammlich GmbH, Pliezhausen
Made in Germany

Published by Gestalten, Berlin 2015
ISBN 978-3-89955-585-1

For more information, please visit www.gestalten.com.

Bibliographic information published by the Deutsche
Nationalbibliothek:
The Deutsche Nationalbibliothek lists this publication in
the Deutsche Nationalbibliografie;
detailed bibliographic data are available online at
http://dnb.d-nb.de.

This book was printed on paper certified according to the
standard of FSC®.